# P. J. O'ROURKE
# NONE
## OF MY
# BUSINESS

**P.J. Explains Money, Banking, Debt, Equity, Assets, Liabilities, and Why He's Not Rich and Neither Are You**

Grove Press
*New York*

Chapters have appeared in a previous version in *American Consequences* and the *Stansberry Digest*

Emoji art design by Erica Leah Wood

*Published simultaneously in Canada*
*Printed in the United States of America*

This book was set in 12.5 point ITC Berkeley Oldstyle by Alpha Design & Composition of Pittsfield, NH

First Grove Atlantic hardcover edition: September 2018
First Grove Atlantic paperback edition: September 2019

Library of Congress Cataloguing-in-Publication data available for this title.

ISBN 978-0-8021-4776-9
eISBN 978-0-8021-4643-4

Grove Press
an imprint of Grove Atlantic
154 West 14th Street
New York, NY 10011

Distributed by Publishers Group West

groveatlantic.com

19  20  21  22    10  9  8  7  6  5  4  3  2  1

To Ed Mallon

Combat veteran, career FBI Agent, business executive, investor, and—best of all—father of my bride

If work was a good thing the rich would have it all
and not let you do it.

—Elmore Leonard, *Split Images*

# CONTENTS

## Section III: Mutant Capitalism

## Section IV: The Transition

## Section V: Consumption

# Foreword

## *Why I'm Not Rich and You Aren't Either*

> To a flock of sheep the sheep who is every evening
> driven by the shepherd into a special pen to feed, and
> becomes twice as fat as the rest, must seem to be a
> genius.
>
> —Leo Tolstoy, *War and Peace*

If you're looking to claw your way up the corporate ladder, succeed beyond your wildest dreams, and amass an enormous fortune, you've got the right book in your hands. Now hit yourself over the head with it.

That stuff doesn't come from books. I *write* books. If wealth came from books I'd be too rich to be writing. I have no idea where power, success, and a big pile of money come from. Probably from someplace awful, such as hard work, or impossible, such as being much smarter than I am.

But it's a lot of fun watching people frantically trying to make—or keep from losing—money. I love economics the way I love the NFL. A great thing about professional football is seeing the guys who stuffed me into my locker in high school break each other's legs. A great thing about economics is how it's like live crabs in a pot of boiling water. If one of them almost makes it out of the pot, the others will pull him back down.

And I say this not as some kind of anticapitalist commie nut, but as a firm believer in the free market and a great fan of economic liberty. I mean, I root for the Patriots. And I root for the Dow Jones too. But, if the guys who hoovered my investment portfolio in the 2008 financial crisis go to bankruptcy court or jail, that's a lot of fun.

Economics is a blood sport that I greatly enjoy—as a spectator. Of course, like everyone else, I am, at some level, a participant in the economy. But I got myself off the field and into a luxury skybox by marrying a woman who was a business major and is much smarter than I am. I leave everything to her. I have no idea what's in my investment portfolio now. I haven't called a play since 2008. It might be a thousand shares of Berkshire Hathaway. It might be a crypto-currency that Jim Cramer pulled out of his ass on *Mad Money*—"Buttcoin." I don't know. I don't want to know. I just want to have fun.

Or I did until the kids got older and I became the father of three adolescents and began to feel that it was incumbent upon me to give them some fatherly advice about how to claw their way up corporate ladders, succeed beyond their wildest dreams, and amass enormous fortunes (with which to take care of me in a luxurious fashion in my old age).

So I told them, "Ask your mother."

Their mother said, "Work hard and be much smarter than your father."

My kids were discouraged by the first part of this advice.

So I tried again. I told them that the best way to do well in life is to find a job that combines what you love to do with what you're good at doing with what people will pay you for. "Take me, for example," I said.

My kids said, *"You?"*

I said, "Well, children, you're not starved to death and naked. Although you . . ." (I said to my eldest daughter) ". . . should wear a sweater over that Forever 21 top. Anyway, I *have* made a living."

And I explained how. I told them. "Think of *What You Love to Do* and *What You're Good at Doing* and *What People Will Pay You for* as three circles. Technically, a Venn diagram. Try to find a place where those three circles intersect, then go there."

And I drew the "Me" diagram on my cocktail napkin.

## ME

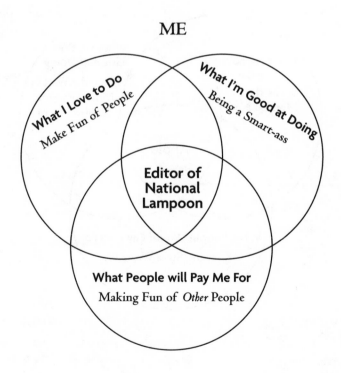

"But, Dad," said my kids, "the *National Lampoon* was, like. forty years ago."

"Right!" I said. "And I'm still riding on its coattails. But I can give you more up-to-date examples."

I mixed another cocktail and got a new napkin.

## Steve Jobs

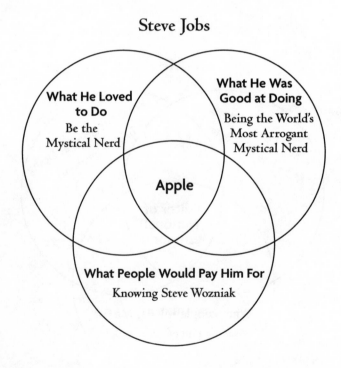

# Bill Gates

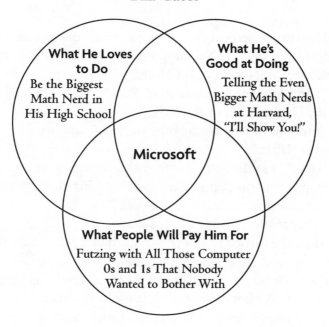

**What He Loves to Do**
Be the Biggest Math Nerd in His High School

**What He's Good at Doing**
Telling the Even Bigger Math Nerds at Harvard, "I'll Show You!"

**Microsoft**

**What People Will Pay Him For**
Futzing with All Those Computer 0s and 1s That Nobody Wanted to Bother With

# Jeff Bezos

**What He Loves to Do**
Rule the World!

**What He's Good at Doing**
Had Boyhood Lemonade Stand That Delivered Lemonade to Your House

**Amazon**

**What People Will Pay Him For**
As It Turns Out, Practically Everything

My wife looked over my shoulder at my doodles and said, "Don't forget, dear, you're supposed to address the NAP-WTF Conference in New York on Monday."

"The 'National Association of People Who Think they're Funny,'" I explained to the kids.

"You'll have to leave by nine o'clock," said my wife. "I've called an Uber."

"Uber?" I said. "Some twerp with a nose ring who plays in a K-pop cover band on weekends driving his mother's Honda Civic. Can't you get me a Yellow Cab?"

"They're out of business," said my wife.

Then she turned to our children. "If you really want to get rich," she said, "listen to your father. Listen especially carefully when he says, 'That'll never catch on.' For example, your father said, 'A phone that connects to the Internet? What for? I've got a computer at home. That'll never catch on.' He said, 'A face-book? Why would anyone want a book full of faces? That'll never catch on.' And he said, 'What the heck is this bird noise, this peeping or cheeping or chirping or twittering I keep hearing about? That'll never catch on.'"

My wife said, "Just listen to your father. And whenever he says, 'That'll never catch on.' *Invest every penny you've got.*"

# SECTION I

## How I Learned Economics by Watching People Try to Kill Each Other

All thy trees and fruit of thy land shall the locusts consume.

—Deuteronomy 28:42

# Introduction

Devoted readers of my books (and I thank you both) will note that there are, in *None of My Business*, certain "Twice-Told Tales." Especially in this section of the work. I have reached the age where I repeat myself. In excuse, I quote that most brahmanic of the Boston Brahmins, Oliver Wendell Holmes, Sr.: "He must be a poor creature who does not often repeat himself. Imagine the author of the excellent piece of advice, 'Know Thyself,' never alluding to that sentiment again."

Not that I have any such excellent piece of advice. My advice is more prosaic: "Know Economics." In pursuit of that knowledge I retell certain adventures that I had over the past thirty-five years as a reporter covering the civil war in Lebanon, the collapse of Albania into anarchy, the perennial anarchy of Somalia, the Iraq War, and a car journey along the Grand Trunk Road from Rawalpindi, Pakistan, to Calcutta on the Bay of Bengal. Then, later in the book, I return to my experiences in Mainland China a dozen years ago and to my other travels through Asia, shifting my reportorial emphasis from war, chaos, and exotic sightseeing to Econ. 101.

I'm trying to explain something, partially to the reader but also to myself. How did a roving hack with—as my friend

Jimmy Buffett once described it—"a phony-baloney job making fun of everything" get interested in economics? Not for nothing did the historian Thomas Carlyle deem economics "the dismal science." It's not the best source of jokes.

This raises another question. How did a phony-baloney wisenheimer get interested in being a foreign correspondent?

I started out, at the beginning of the 1970s, as a cub wisenheimer at the *National Lampoon*, making fun of everything. When I became a freelancer in the early 1980s, I started to look around for something specific to make fun of, to establish my "professional niche." I settled on foreigners as my topic. Everybody loves making fun of foreigners. But no one had set out to do it for a living since the heyday of the British Empire.

> *Alas! What various tastes in food*
> *Divide the human brotherhood!*
> *Birds in their little nests agree*
> *With Chinamen, but not with me.*
> *Colonials like their oysters hot,*
> *Their omelets heavy—I do not.*
> *The French are fond of slugs and frogs,*
> *The Siamese eat puppy-dogs . . .*
> *In Italy the traveler notes*
> *With great disgust the flesh of goats*
> *Appearing on the table d'hôtes;*
> *And even this the natives spoil*
> *By frying it in rancid oil.*
> —Hilaire Belloc

Making fun of international shenanigans (and silly foreign cuisine) soon led to making fun of the politics that underlay the shenanigans. And one cannot inspect politics at close range for long without overturning the rock of economics and making fun of the squirmy, slimy things that live there.

No matter what armed imbroglio, conflict, crisis, or catastrophe I was writing about, everybody was in it for something. Me, of course: I wanted good copy. But everybody else wanted to profit from the situation too. Perhaps the profit would be in money. Perhaps the profit would be in power. Perhaps the profit would be in pride or renown. The most virtuous people involved were piling up treasure in heaven. The most helpless people hoped to profit merely by staying alive.

Some read about economics on their own. Some take economics in college. Others are students at a tougher school, the Academy of Feeding a Family. I followed a different path.

I filed stories for *Rolling Stone*, *The Atlantic Monthly*, and *The Weekly Standard* from forty-some countries, none of them the nice ones. I reported on wars, revolutions, coups, riots, civil disturbances, persecutions, oppressions, and other human unpleasantness. My job, phony-baloney as it may have been, was, basically to watch people try to kill each other.

Watching people try to kill each other teaches important economic lessons.

# Lesson I:
# The Power of the
# Economic Impulse

The first time I went to a war zone was in 1984 during the Lebanese Civil War. I flew to Beirut on Middle East Airlines. MEA, the Lebanese national flag-carrier, had a flight schedule that, somehow, was never interrupted by the war. Looking back, I should have realized that all sides in that multifarious conflict were making payoffs to MEA. Everybody needed a way to get money, combatants, warlords, spies, and other personnel into (and out of) the country they were tearing apart.

Just stepping off the airplane showed me what a good job of it they were doing.

The airport windows were shattered. The fronds were blown off the palm trees in the parking lot. The surrounding streets were pitch dark; all the lampposts had been run over by tanks. The taxi I got into looked like it had been used by Steve McQueen for a POW breakout attempt in *The Great Escape*.

Getting into the city from the airport meant negotiating a dozen checkpoints controlled by different militias from Lebanon's various warring factions. At each checkpoint militiamen would brandish their weapons and shout at me: "Bassboat!" "Passboot!" "Pisspot!"

What they wanted was my passport, the one English word that every militiaman knew and none of them could pronounce.

I finally got to the Commodore Hotel, the unofficial HQ of the foreign press in Lebanon. The smiling bell clerk asked, "Would you like a room on the car-bomb side of the hotel or on the mortar-shell side?" I had to empty the minibar to get to sleep.

The Lebanese Civil War lasted from 1975 until 1990. It started as a conflict between the Christian Lebanese, who were the majority of the politicians, and the Muslim Lebanese, who were the majority of the population.

In 1975 and 1976 the center of Beirut—"The Paris of the Middle East," with its cafés, nightclubs, luxury hotels, and beachfront Corniche—was reduced to rubble. Thousands of people died. The country's government collapsed. And—the Mideast being the Mideast—things got worse after that.

The Sunni Muslim Lebanese began fighting the Shia Muslim Lebanese. The Islamic fundamentalist Lebanese began fighting the Islamic secularist Lebanese. The Palestinian refugees living in Lebanon began fighting the Druze, a Lebanese sect that's an offshoot of Islam. Then Syria invaded one end of Lebanon and Israel invaded the other.

There's not room here to explain it all. There's not room *anywhere* to explain it all.

Anyway, by the time I got to Lebanon the place was a complete mess. Economics was not on my mind. I was reporting on war and the political, religious, and ethnic issues behind the fighting. At the time, it didn't occur to me that Lebanon *had* an economy.

Of course, Lebanon did have an economy—otherwise all the Lebanese who weren't dead from the civil war would have been dead from starvation.

Actually, Lebanon had a remarkable economy. In the midst of murderous chaos, the Lebanese economy continued to function. Considering the circumstances, you could even say it thrived.

True, the war led to runaway inflation, as wars do. A U.S. dollar was worth three Lebanese pounds in 1975; by 1992, $1 U.S. bought 2,500 pounds. But this didn't bother the Lebanese. They conducted business in British pounds, French francs, U.S. dollars, or whatever hard currency came to hand. Children selling cigarettes in the street would give you that day's international exchange rate.

Beirut was loud, but not with the din of battle. The city's electrical grid had been destroyed, so every business and home had a portable gasoline generator on the sidewalk with extension cords snaking every which way. The generators were noisy enough to drown out all but the loudest gunfire.

Fuel seemed as plentiful as ammunition. Traffic was heavy and the driving was erratic. It always is in the Mideast, but more so when the stoplights don't work, the traffic cops are in hiding, and drivers are dodging sniper fire.

Shops were open, including shops selling things you wouldn't think would have a wartime market. Few journalists returned from Beirut without an acre of Persian carpets: "Special war price."

The Commodore Hotel did a brisk business, especially its bar, where the press corps sought treatment for post- (and pre-post-) traumatic stress disorder.

Lebanon produces good wine. Chateau Musar, vintage 1975, was in great demand. It was in such great demand that an amazing number of bottles of Musar '75 were for sale—so many that the Chateau Musar vineyard must occupy most of Lebanon's landmass, and 1975 must have lasted ten years.

The Muslim militia controlling the neighborhood around the Commodore opposed alcohol and invaded bars and sprayed the wine racks and liquor shelves with machine-gun fire. But some kind of deal had been arranged at the Commodore. The Commodore's bar was invaded once, for form's sake, I guess. But a timely forewarning meant that no bottles of Musar '75 were machine-gunned, just Coke and Fanta.

Where the money for all this economic activity came from, I don't know. Well, I do know. When I visited Lebanon's fertile agricultural area, the Bekaa Valley, the fields were full as far as the eye could see with lush, tall green marijuana plants.

The Lebanese Civil War caused terrible losses. More than 250,000 people were killed or wounded—10 percent of the prewar population. Nearly a million people were displaced. Property damage was incalculable. But one thing the Lebanese did not lose was their economic impulse.

While I was working on my article about the civil war, I went to the southern suburbs of Beirut to interview people about the political, religious, and ethnic issues that led to the fighting. I was stopped at a Hezbollah checkpoint (the same Hezbollah that's fighting in Syria now).

Hezbollah's checkpoints were manned (I should say "boyed") by fourteen- and fifteen-year-olds with AK-47s. They twirled their weapons around, poked them in the dirt, and scratched their ears with the muzzle sights. Gun safety merit badges must go begging in the Lebanese Boy Scouts.

"Bassboat!" shouted the adolescent at this checkpoint. When he saw my American passport, he was furious. He stuck the AK-47's barrel inches from my nose.

The teenager spoke some English. He subjected me to a twenty-minute tirade about "Great American Satan Devil." I was berated at gunpoint for how America had caused war, famine, injustice, poverty, and Zionism all over the world.

At last the boy finished his rant. He lowered his gun and gave me back my passport. Then he said, in a normal tone of voice, "As soon as I am getting my green card I am going to Dearborn, Michigan, to study dentist school."

Bless the power of the economic impulse. Today that kid's probably a wealthy orthodontist living in Bloomfield Hills. And I'll bet he votes Republican.

# Lesson 2:
# The Real Secret Behind
# All Investment Scams

In 1997 I went to Albania to cover the complete collapse of the Albanian economy and, hence, of Albania.

The collapse was caused by investment scams. The scams were simple pyramid, or "Ponzi," schemes. Scammers promised foolishly high investment returns. Foolish investors were paid off with money from more foolish investors. The more foolish were paid off with money from the more foolish yet.

The "greater fool theory" indicates this can go on forever. No matter how idiotic you are there are bigger idiots out there.

Mathematics, however, indicates this cannot go on forever. If a pyramid scheme grows in an exponential manner—$10^1$, $10^2$, $10^3$, etc.—it takes just ten layers of a pyramid to include nearly twice the population of earth.

The population of Albania was 3.2 million. And, as far as I was able to tell, all of them had invested in pyramid schemes.

We know what happens with pyramid schemes. Charles Ponzi's hoax about arbitrage of international postal coupons fizzled in 1920. Bernie Madoff's hoax about sailing above market fluctuations flopped in 2008. Ponzi's and Madoff's investors were outraged.

But not as outraged as Albanians. There were violent protests. The government banned public meetings. The protests became more violent. The army was ordered to shoot. All the soldiers deserted.

The soldiers had money in the pyramid schemes too. They were as angry as anyone else. The violent protests turned into armed rebellions. Albania's military arsenal was looted. There was a lot to loot.

Until 1992 Albania was controlled by fanatical Stalinists. Albania was as isolated and bellicose as the only other country it had diplomatic relations with, North Korea. The Albanian military was armed with 1.5 million rifles, pistols, and machine guns—all stolen along with 10.5 billion rounds of ammunition.

Heavy weapons were also pilfered. The National Commercial Bank in the city of Gjirokaster was robbed with a tank.

Theft slipped into pillage. The railroad to Montenegro was stolen—the track torn up and sold for scrap. Pillage degenerated into vandalism. Schools, museums, and hospitals were wrecked. And vandalism reached heroic scale. Bridges were demolished, water-supply pumping stations were blown up, power lines and telephone wires were pulled down. Albania came to bits.

I got through on one of the few remaining phones to the only remaining hotel in Albania's capital, Tirana, and took the one remaining weekly flight from Italy.

The hotel sent a driver and translator, Elmaz, in an old Mercedes belonging to who-knows-whom. There were no customs formalities or security checks at the Tirana airport. How could anything or anybody be more dangerous than what was in Albania already?

Albania came to bits, but not to a standstill. The crumbling two-lane road into town was full of cars, trucks, and horse carts loaded with all sorts of things belonging to who-knows-whom.

More cars and trucks, crashed or abandoned, lined the road. Albania had so many wrecked and stolen cars that the horse carts were all fitted with automobile seats, some with center consoles and luxurious upholstery.

Elmaz was studying to be a veterinarian. Everything had been stolen from his school—books, drugs, lab equipment, even parts of the buildings themselves. "We are without windows, without doors," said Elmaz. "We study with only desks and walls."

The desks had been stolen too, but the faculty found them in a local flea market and bought them back. "All the horses we had were shot, "said Elmaz.

An American wire-service reporter at the hotel bar said of the locals, "They'll rob you." The moment he said that a neophyte British television producer limped in and told us he'd just lost a car, a TV camera, and $5,000.

The first Albanian pyramid scheme was Sijdia Holdings, offering 5 or 6 percent interest a month. Sijdia Holdings had some real assets. Its founder, Hadjim Sijdia, was jailed in Switzerland for fraud but got out and somehow managed to repay his debts. This lent credence to nine other large pyramid schemes. That, in turn, led to a plethora of mini-pyramids, some offering interest as high as 50 percent a month.

"My family had two thousand dollars in the pyramid schemes," said Elmaz. It was their entire savings.

I interviewed an Albanian newspaper editor, Ilir Nishku. He said, "The pyramid schemes created the idea that this is the free market and just four years after communism we could get rich. They created the wrong idea that *this* is capitalism"

Albania's economic statistics looked great: 9.6 percent growth in 1993, 8.3 in 1994, 13.3 in 1995, 9.1 in 1996. And that should tell us something about the gullibility—or the stupidity or, maybe, the corruption—of the people who compile economic statistics.

The *United Nations 1996 Human Development Report* declared that Albania's "progress in wide-spread economic well-being . . . has continued, forming a social basis for human development."

"Everyone was sitting in cafés," said Elmaz.

Then, in February 1997, five of the nine large pyramid schemes and all of the small ones failed. The remaining four quit paying interest and froze account withdrawals. An estimated $1.5 billion disappeared—half the Albanian GDP.

That's what usually happens. Even in America, where we have excellent legal and financial systems—excellent by Albanian standards—Bernie Madoff's investors lost billions. After ten years of searching for Madoff's assets, $6 billion is still missing.

Albania is different from America. Albania is more desperate, more violent, less orderly. But those are quantitative differences. Are there qualitative differences? Were Albanians putting their money into pyramid schemes really different from Americans bankrolling Charles Ponzi or giving their money to Bernie Madoff to manage?

I went to Albania to learn why the country had been so vulnerable to pyramid schemes. How could a whole nation be, essentially, destroyed by a chain letter?

It took me less than an hour to find out.

The first thing Elmaz did was take me to meet editor Nishku. The first thing I asked Nishku was, "Why were the pyramids so popular in Albania? Were people just unsophisticated about money after all those years of Communist isolation?"

"No," he said. "There had been pyramid schemes already elsewhere in Eastern Europe, and they had collapsed before the Albanian ones were started. People in Albania knew about such things."

"Then how," I asked, "did so many Albanians get suckered in?"

"They knew," Nishku said, "so much money could not be made honestly. They thought there was smuggling and money laundering involved to make these great profits."

Herein the lesson. The Albanians didn't believe they were victims of a scam. They believed they were the perpetrators.

# Lesson 3:
# (Topic for Discussion)
# If You Want Hard Money,
# How Hard Do You
# Have to Be to Get It?

We worry about our currency, the kind of money we use, our medium of exchange.

Precious metals are a reliable long-term store of value. But they're cumbersome. You don't want to fall into the swimming pool at the senior living community with your pockets full of your retirement savings in one-ounce gold Canadian Maple Leaf coins.

"Fiduciary money"—certificates bearing a government promise to redeem paper currency for precious metals—presents different problems. Governments lie about having those precious metals. And governments do worse than lie. People holding fiduciary money can wake up—as they did on April 5, 1933, when FDR signed Executive Order 6102 banning the ownership of gold—to find out that redeeming the certificates for what the law says they're worth is against the law.

Then there's "fiat currency," backed by nothing at all and spilling out of government printing presses in sheets, quires, reams, and bales. The reason it's supposed to be worth something is the "Lousy Parenting Reason." A frustrated and inept government tells us, like we frustrated and inept parents tell our children, *"Because I said so!"*

Maybe bitcoin is the answer. But nobody really understands bitcoin. To most of us, bitcoin seems like a weird scam invented by strange geeks with weaponized slide rules in the high school Evil Math Club.

So we worry about our currency. And we worry that if our currency collapses, our society will collapse.

Maybe one way to understand currency collapse is to go someplace where society has collapsed already.

I went to Somalia in 1992 to cover "Operation Restore Hope," the U.S.-led military mission to save Somalia— notionally from famine, actually from itself.

I have some experience with what's called "anarchy." I've just described my experiences in Lebanon during its civil war and in Albania when its pyramid schemes went kerflooey.

But the war in Lebanon *was* a war, and wars, however multisided and confusing, always have an organizing principle.

And what happened in Albania was stealing. Stealing comes to an end when everything's been stolen. Today Albania is a typical little Eastern European country—a member of NATO and an applicant for EU membership with 3 million tourists a year and a per capita gross national income of $11,880 (nearly twice that of India).

Somalia was true anarchy. A vicious dictator, Siad Barre, had been overthrown and the Somalis celebrated their independence by shooting each other.

Fighting broke out everywhere. It wasn't traditional Africa tribal warfare—the Somalis all belong to the same tribe. But the tribe has six clans, the six clans have hundreds of subclans, and each subclan is divided into infinite murderous feuds.

The Somalis fought each other with rifles, machine guns, mortars, cannons and—to judge by the look of Mogadishu—wads of filth.

In the old town not one stone stood upon another. In the new part of the city everything was built out of concrete, and the concrete had been blasted back into piles of aggregate, rebar, and Portland cement.

There was no water and no electricity. At night the only illumination was from tracer bullets. Every tree and bush had been snatched for firewood. Sewage welled up through what pavement was left. Mounds of sand blew through the streets. Rubbish was dumped atop wreckage and goats grazed on the offal.

Everything that guns can accomplish had been achieved in Mogadishu.

I signed on as a radio reporter with a U.S. broadcast network; Somalia wasn't someplace I could go on my own. When I arrived at Mogadishu in a chartered Cessna the first thing I encountered were armed Somalis. Fortunately they were the network's armed Somalis, bodyguards hired to do things like keep me from being robbed and shot.

The network—presumably with the help of the U.S. military—had found a walled mansion, more or less intact, near the airport.

Some thirty of us—reporters, camera crews, video editors, producers, and tech guys—were housed in this compound, bedded down in shifts while our forty-man army of Somali mercenaries camped in the courtyard.

It was impossible for us to go outside our walls without a truckful of "security" (as the Somali mercenaries liked to be called). Even with our gunmen along there were always people massing up to beg and thieve. Hands tugged at wallet pockets. Fingers nipped at wristwatch bands. No foreigner could make a move without attracting a hornet's nest of attention—demanding, grasping, pushing mobs of cursing, whining, sneering people. Young men waving AK-47 assault rifles pushed among the crowd. Rusted, dent-covered, wind-shield-less pickup trucks with gun mounts welded into their beds sputtered by on predatory errands.

Our big job as reporters was to cover President George H. W. Bush's New Year's visit to the American troops in Somalia.

President Bush also decided to visit a Somali orphanage in Baidoa, a small city 160 miles of bad road away from Moga-dishu. The president traveled by helicopter. We were not so lucky.

Broadcasting the president's visit required a Land Rover full of reporters and another full of technicians plus two trail-ers, one carrying a satellite dish and another loaded with a generator. Somali "security" were needed to guard these—two truckloads in front of us and a truckload behind.

On our way to Baidoa we were escorted by U.S. Marines. The trip was uneventful. The trip back was not. The Marines had stayed in Baidoa.

A dozen impromptu roadblocks had been set up by the locals. These were lengths of iron pipe balanced on an oil drum and counterweighted with a chunk of concrete. One harmless-looking old fellow squatted at each roadblock. He was not asking for a toll. You could see what the deal was when you stood on the Land Rover seat and looked out the sunroof at the surrounding thornbush. Armed creeps lurked.

If you had more guns than the creeps the harmless-looking fellow raised the pole and obsequiously waved you through. If you did not have more guns you were robbed and shot. We had more guns.

But then we got a flat tire. The flat occurred where the thornbush was thick, providing an uncomfortable amount of creep cover.

It took some convincing to get our Somalis out of their trucks and into a semblance of a perimeter while the tech guys changed the tire.

We had plenty of guns. The problem was the fellows wielding them. Aside from the question of whether our hired Somalis were trustworthy (a good question), some of them did not need to shave yet. I walked around to the back of our convoy and the "security" standing solitary guard there was maybe 4-foot-10, possibly weighed 90 pounds, and was straining to keep his AK at port arms. I took the gun from the kid and stood guard myself. I am not a fearsome-looking man. But SpongeBob SquarePants would have been fearsome compared with our miniature Tail End Charlie.

Thus I came to understand that there's always a currency, there's always a medium of exchange. And, although I haven't been back to Somalia since 1993, I know from the news that the Somali medium of exchange has not lost any value in the past twenty-two years.

A few days after I got back from Baidoa another reporter, whom I'll call Leon, and I decided to go to downtown Mogadishu, or what was left of it, just to have a look around. We went with an armed Somali driver, an armed Somali translator, and the requisite truckful of security.

But, nonetheless, Leon was carrying a 9mm Glock. When we got out of the car Leon held the Glock above his head and racked a round into the pistol's chamber with a dramatic flourish.

Leon turned to me and said, "I call it the Visa card of the future."

# SECTION II

## Money and Banking
### *You Can Take This to the . . . Whatever*

The progress of the enormous debts which
at present oppress, and will in the long-run
probably ruin, all the great nations of Europe,
has been pretty uniform . . . When national debts
have once been accumulated to a certain degree,
there is scarce, I believe, a single instance of their
having been fairly and completely paid.

—Adam Smith, *The Wealth of Nations*


I was much further out than you thought
And not waving but drowning.

—Stevie Smith, "Not Waving but Drowning"

# Introduction

In addition to the nightmare that is money—and I'll get to that in a moment—there is the horrible thing called banking.

Specifically, the horrible thing is called "fractional-reserve banking." This is the kind of banking that's practiced everywhere in the sophisticated, cosmopolitan world, where people are too polite to shout, "Show me the money!" (The rest of the world, quite sensibly, operates on a cash-on-the-barrelhead basis.)

Although we know better, at a subconscious level we all have an image of banks as being like Scrooge McDuck's money vault. We put our money in banks, and bankers put that money—all those ones and fives and dimes and quarters—into a great big safe, where they rub it and dust it and stack it in piles, and where sometimes, late at night, the bankers take off all their clothes and roll in the stuff and yell, "Whee!"

In fact, banks don't keep any money. Money is kept only in ATM machines. (No one knows where this money comes from. But somehow wives always find out whom it goes to on husbands' "business trips.")

All banks keep in their great big safes are a few Sacagawea dollars and a stack of twenties with an exploding dye pellet to give to bank robbers.

This is why your bank is always urging you to "bank on-line." That way you'll never notice that there isn't any money in the bank. And, what with "online banking automatic bill payment" (whether you want to pay the bill or not), you won't have any money in the bank anyway.

Banks are required to keep only a "fractional reserve" of the money that you put into them. The rest of your money is then available for the bank to loan to such creditors as college students in the ninth semester of their junior year, credit card bingers who've just spent their annual income on a lifetime supply of figet spinners, and buyers of used cars from dealers whose credit rating checks are so sketchy that every car they sell comes with a repo man in the trunk.

Under the system of fractional reserve banking, the fraction of your money that the bank has to keep in the bank can be (depending on what Republicans have been up to with banking regulations lately) as small as %. Possibly less.

Each bank has a certain "capital requirement"—a minimum net worth—that it has to maintain to stay in business. But all sorts of things can be included, on paper, to raise that capital requirement to the necessary regulatory level. For instance, the bank counts the money that you've deposited in the bank as part of its capital even though it owes you the money. The bank counts its shareholder equity and retained earnings as part of its capital (like anybody is ever going to see those again). It counts the bank building and the land under the parking lot. And—my favorite—the bank counts something called "subordinated debt."

Subordinated debt is not money that the bank has. It's money that the bank has borrowed from somebody else, maybe you. In other words, the money that you have deposited in a bank is guaranteed by money that you've loaned the bank plus money that you've deposited in the bank, which the bank owes you back, plus a parking lot.

Hello, mattress. Meet my savings.

# The Strange, Shape-Shifting Symbol of Value

Money isn't the root of all evil. Money is the root of *everything*.

What money is is necessary. Necessary for good stuff. Necessary for bad stuff. Necessary for all the stuff that comes in between—the stuff of life.

But what money also is is very hard to comprehend. Why's this soiled, crumpled, overdecorated piece of paper bearing a picture of a man who was something of a failure as a president worth $50? Meanwhile, why's this clean, soft, white, and cleverly folded piece of paper worth so little that I just blew my nose on it?

And it's not just me who's confused. All the world's top economists, powerful central bankers, and leading politicians seem to lack a basic conceptual understanding of money.

What exactly is a "dollar"?

If it's a thing that I want, why do I prefer to have fifty grimy old dollars instead of one nice new one? This isn't true of other things—like puppies, for instance.

Of course, money is not a puppy. Money is not a specific thing. Money is a symbol of things in general, a symbol of how much you want things, and a symbol of how many things you're going to get. Money is an abstract representation of value.

But what is *value*? The brief answer is, "It's complicated." Value varies according to time, place, circumstance, and whether or not the puppy ruined the rug.

Plus, some things are difficult to place a value on. This is why we don't use money to measure all of our exchanges. Kids get food, clothing, and shelter from parents. And in return, parents get . . . kids.

Important emotional, moral, and legal distinctions are made between sex and paying for sex, even if the socially approved kind of sex costs a dinner and a movie.

We need economic goods all the time, but we don't always need money for them. And that's a good thing, since for most of human existence, there wasn't any money at all.

In ancient times, money didn't exist. Or rather, everything that existed was money. If I sold you a cow for six goats, you were charging it on your Goat Card.

Anything that's used to measure value, if it has value itself, is "commodity money." Societies that didn't have dollar bills picked one or two commodities as proto-greenbacks.

The Aztecs used cocoa beans for money, North Africans used salt (the origin of the word "salary"), and medieval Norwegians used butter and dried cod. (Their ATMs were a mess.)

Some commodities work better as money than others. Celebrities would make bad money. Carrying a couple around would be a bother, and you would have to hack a leg off to make change.

Precious metals, however, make good money and have been used that way for more than five thousand years.

Metal commodity money is portioned out by weight. A commodity money coin is just a hunk of precious metal stamped to indicate how much it weighs.

Moving from weighing money to stamping coins is a simple step, but a couple thousand years passed before the step was taken. Nobody trusted anybody else to do the stamping.

When coins *were* invented, the distrust proved to be well-founded. The first Western coins were minted by the kingdom of Lydia, in what is now Turkey. They were made of a gold-silver alloy called electrum.

It's hard for anyone but a chemist (and there weren't any) to tell how much gold is in a piece of electrum versus how much silver. The king of Lydia, Croesus, became proverbial for his wealth.

In China, the weight of bronze "cash" was supposed to be guaranteed by death penalties. A lot of people must have gone to the electric chair (or would have if the Chinese had had electricity).

A horse cost 4,500 "one cash" coins during the Han dynasty (206 B.C to 220 A.D.) and 25,000 cash during the Tang dynasty (618 A.D. to 907).

It's very hard for the people who issue cash to resist the temptation to debase that cash.

Kings, emperors, and even lowly congressional representatives have expenses. It is to a government's advantage to pay for those expenses with funny money.

One reason that the concept of money so often violates common sense is that governments so often do crazy things with money.

Another reason that money violates common sense is that we don't have to use real commodities as money. We can use pieces of paper promising to deliver those real commodities. This is "fiduciary money," from the Latin word *fiducia*, meaning "trust."

In Europe, paper money was developed privately, in the thirteenth century, from bills of exchange traded among Italian merchants and from receipts given by goldsmiths to whom precious metals had been entrusted for safekeeping.

Public fiduciary money was first printed in Sweden. Swedish commodity money came in the form of copper plates. Thus, in Sweden, a large fortune was a *large* fortune.

In 1656, the Stockholms Banco began issuing more convenient paper notes. The bank issued too many notes, and the Swedish government went broke.

In 1716, Scotsman John Law helped the French government establish the Banque Royale, issuing notes backed by the value of France's land holdings west of the Mississippi. Banque Royale issued too many notes, and the French government went broke.

The largest Western experiment with fiduciary money took place right here in America. In 1775 the Second Continental Congress not only created paper money, but passed a law against refusing to accept it. The Continental Congress issued too many notes and . . . A pattern begins to emerge.

All fiduciary money is backed by a commodity, even if the backers are lying about the amount of that commodity.

Historically, the commodity most often chosen has been gold. By the nineteenth century, the major currencies of the world were based on gold, led by the most major currency among them, the British pound.

This was a period of monetary stability and, not coincidentally, great economic growth. Some people think we should go back on the gold standard, and not all of them have skinny sideburns and large belt buckles and live on armed compounds in Idaho. Money ought to be worth *something*, and gold seems as good as anything.

But the relationship between money and value is endlessly perplexing. The high value of gold is a social convention, a habit left over from the days when bright, unblemished things (people included) were rare.

Gold may go out of fashion. A generation may come along that regards gold as gross or immoral, the way millennials regard veal.

And gold is a product. We may discover different methods to get huge new amounts of it.

This happened to the Spanish. When they conquered the New World, they obtained tons of gold, melted it down, and sent it to the mint. It never occurred to them that they were just creating more money, not more things to spend it on. Between 1500 and 1600, prices in Spain went up 400 percent.

Instead of the vast wealth of America's oceans, fields, and forests, Spain took the gold. It was as if someone robbed a bank and stole nothing but deposit slips.

Gold is not an absolutely, perfectly rational basis for a currency. But the real problem with fiduciary money—from a government standpoint—is that it's inconvenient.

A currency that can be converted into a commodity limits the amount of currency that can be printed. A government has to have at least some of the commodity or the world makes a laughingstock out of its banknotes—"not worth a Continental."

So if a government can lie about the amount of a commodity that is backing its currency—the way the Stockholms Banco, Banque Royale, and Second Continental Congress did—why can't a government lie about everything?

Instead of passing a law saying one dollar equals X amount of gold, why not pass a law saying one dollar equals one dollar? This is "fiat money," from the Latin word for "a binding edict." And fiat money is almost the only kind of national currency left in the world.

Fiat money is backed by nothing but faith that a government won't keep printing money until we're using it in place of something more valuable, such as Kleenex.

Concerning this faith, the experiences of Weimar's Germany, Carter's America, Yeltsin's Russia, etc., make agnostics of us all.

The only thing that protects us from completely worthless money is our ability to buy and sell. We can move our stock of wealth from the imaginary value of dollars to the fictitious value of euros to the mythical value of stock shares to the illusory value of real estate, and so forth.

Our freedom to not use a particular kind of money keeps the issuers of that money . . . "honest" wouldn't be the word but somewhat *moderate* in their dishonesty. Or it used to.

Money is a symbol of value, but it's a symbol that's strange, shape-shifting, and hard to define. And value is something that's personal and relative, and changes from moment to moment.

Money can't always be valued. And value can't always be priced. And this is the price we pay for money.

# My Own Personal
# Central Bank

Many "classical liberal" and libertarian economists are skeptical about the Central Banks that issue fiat money. Not me. I like them. I want one.

Of course, I don't want an enormous Central Bank like the Federal Reserve. Where would I put it? And, although we live in a big old house in the country, we don't have enough bedrooms to host seven Federal Reserve Board governors and twelve Reserve Bank presidents at those Federal Open Market Committee meetings they're always having. We'd have to put some of them in the hayloft. (Do they bring their families?) Plus we'd have to feed them. I hope FOMC members are okay with weenies and burgers on the grill and a cooler full of beer.

No, what I want is a compact household-size type of Central Bank for my own personal use. A small, handy "Central Bank of O'Rourke" that would fit in the laundry room or in the mudroom between the dog kennels.

The reason I want my own Central Bank is that I've been reading up on the Federal Reserve Act of 1913 and the mandate it gave to the Federal Reserve Bank—specifically, the mandate as it was amended during the 1970s and '80s in "Section 2A. Monetary policy objectives."

I have two monetary policy objectives:

Monetary objective: Get rich.
Policy objective: Stay rich.

Therefore, I was interested to see what Section 2A had to say, which I quote in the paragraph below, with my own comments in brackets.

The Board of Governors of the Federal Reserve System and the Federal Open Market Committee shall maintain long run growth of the monetary and credit aggregates [e.g., the O'Rourke checking account balance and Visa card credit limit] commensurate with the [my] economy's long run potential to increase production [maybe someone will turn one of my books into a hit movie], so as to promote effectively the goals of maximum employment [I could do without "maximum employment," but I've got three kids to put through college so it's not like I've got a choice], stable prices [especially for the shoes and clothes my wife and daughters shop for on the Internet], and moderate long-term interest rates [on the credit card debt to pay for shoes and clothes].

My kind of mandate!

But there's a problem with getting the United States Federal Reserve Bank to exercise its mandate on my individual behalf and help me reach my particular monetary policy objectives: I have to stand in line.

The Federal Reserve is a large establishment for use by the general public—kind of like the men's room at Penn Station in New York. And, kind of like the men's room at Penn Station, all sorts of stuff goes on inside the Fed that I don't want anything to do with, such as mopping up government deficits and pissing on free enterprise.

I prefer a private facility. In fact, I prefer a private everything—private railroad car, private jet, private tropical island. But these are expensive. According to what I've read about the history of central banking, a private Central Bank would seem to have a zero purchase price and virtually no maintenance costs.

(An extremely condensed history of central banking: In 1694 British King William III was fighting the Nine Years' War with France and ran out of money in about Year One. He said, "Let's have a Bank of England to borrow some from." The Chancellor of the Exchequer, Charles Montagu, First Earl of Halifax, said, "Jolly good idea." And Bob's your uncle.)

Most of what a Central Bank does is so-called open market operations. These consist of buying bonds from a government. In this case I'm the government. I have any number of "PJ Treasuries," "P-Bills," "J-Notes," etc., all neatly hand-lettered on my personalized stationery and available in denominations up to $1 godzillion with maturities ranging from "After-I'm-dead" to "When-hell-freezes-over."

A Central Bank pays for bonds by issuing currency. I'll use the color Xerox down at the copy store. It's not counterfeiting when a Central Bank does it.

Of course, my Central Bank will need to be a "politically independent" institution, the way the Federal Reserve is. The President of the United States can't just tell the chairman of the Federal Reserve what to do.

On the other hand, the president *does* appoint the Fed chairman, and the Fed governors, too. I'm going to appoint my dogs—Clio, Georgie, and Bodey. They're very cute dogs, so I don't foresee any problems with Senate confirmation.

(Senators rejecting cute dogs, would cause a furious national outcry on Facebook and Twitter.)

I assure you, my dogs are *very* independent. If I tell them, "Sit," or "Stay," or "Come," they just look at me with dull incomprehension and keep on chasing squirrels. And yet I think I can persuade them to give me a unanimous bark of approval for pursuing my monetary policy objectives . . . *"Clio, Georgie, Bodey—want a treat?!"*

Now, what else can I get my Central Bank to do for me?

A Central Bank manages the currency and money supply of a nation. In this case that's the United States of Me. I'm headed back to the Xerox machine at the copy shop right now.

A Central Bank also manages a nation's interest rates. There are a number of different interest rates that a Central Bank manages—target rate, nominal rate, effective rate, discount rate. Therefore my Central Bank will manage interest rates so that I, too, have a variety to choose from.

There's that ultralow rate on my Visa card balance that I mentioned before. But in other situations I'd like other rates. No more .4 percent 6-month CDs, please. The Reserve Bank of O'Rourke will make sure that the return on my savings account falls somewhere between Venezuela government bond yields and Mafia loan-shark vigorish.

My Central Bank can take care of this, because another thing Central Banks do is oversee commercial banks.

And my local bank could use a little oversight. Next time I go there I'll bring Georgie, the chairman of my Fed. Georgie is an adorable black Lab, but she also has teeth like a set of steak knives and a deep and fearsome growl.

Then I'll explain to the bank manager that when I balanced my checkbook, yes, I did *add* a $1,220 check I wrote to my previous balance of $980 instead of *subtracting* the $1,220 from the $980. But that's what a government does with "off-budget" spending involving such programs as Medicare, which I'm on. Therefore, using official U.S. federal government–approved budget math, I now have $2,200 in my checking account, not -$240. And Georgie will provide oversight by going, *"Grrrrr . . ."*

That being one more thing Central Banks do—facilitate government debt and deficits. In fact, harking back to King Billy in 1694, that's *all* Central Banks do.

But I've got plenty of debt and deficits already and don't need any more.

Also note that, per King Billy, the debt and deficits always seem to be used to finance bad ideas such as a Nine Years' War with France. Or, nowadays, massive entitlement programs that devastate the work ethic, destroy family ties, and strip people of their personal responsibility and self-respect. In my case the debt and deficits would probably finance a Harley-Davidson. I'm too old to be riding one. The Harley would quickly turn me into a "rolling organ donor."

I'm beginning to reconsider whether having my own personal Central Bank is such a good idea after all.

The main difference between governments and individuals is that governments have Central Banks and individuals don't. The other main difference between governments and individuals is that governments are stupider. This is because governments have Central Banks to fund their stupidity.

Individuals are forced to be "fiscal conservatives." If we become ridiculously indebted far beyond our ability to repay, we lose the house, the car, *and* the Harley.

Individuals are required to have a sensible "macroeconomic policy." It's fine for the Fed to ruin whole sectors of the economy by creating an immense pool of assets that exist only on paper. When an individual does that he's Bernie Madoff.

Individuals are constrained by a cautious and moderate "foreign policy." An individual can't afford to invade a neighbor's home. He'll be shot (especially up here in rural New England where I live).

Individuals don't have the assets to damage the social fabric with public policies that turn inner cities into war zones. The only individuals who have those kinds of assets are drug lords, and they get arrested. Or at least I hope they do.

So . . . I wonder. If I had my own Central Bank and the unlimited power that an unlimited amount of money would give me, would I start to be as stupid as a government?

What's to stop me?

# Negative Interest Rates— Not Only Wrong but Evil

Oh, for the good old days when banks adhered to the "3-6-3 Rule"—pay depositors 3 percent, charge borrowers 6 percent, play golf at 3.

Instead, as of this writing, we have a European Central Bank interest rate of 0 percent and Central Bank interest rates that are worse than zero in Japan (-0.10), Sweden (-0.50), Denmark (-0.65), and Switzerland (-0.75).

WTF? Let Bloomberg News explain: "Negative interest rates are an act of desperation, a signal that traditional policy options have proved ineffective and new limits need to be explored. They punish banks that hoard cash instead of extending loans. Policy makers in both Europe and Japan are trying to shield their economies from deflation, or a spiral of falling prices that could derail the recovery."

These interest rates are not only desperate, *they're immoral*.

The old-fashioned term for borrowing was "renting money." And that's the way central bankers should start thinking about it again. A sum of money is a thing, a piece of property, like a house.

When a government agency decrees a 0 percent interest rate, this is the same as the government forcing you to rent a house you own for nothing.

And what kind of tenant will you get for the price of bupkis-per-month? You'll get somebody running a meth lab— if you're lucky.

Of course, you'll still have to pay the upkeep on your rental property. In the case of money, this means paying the taxes on what you've earned and saved so that you can have a sum of money to rent to someone.

Between the cost of "maintenance" on your money and the cost of inflation lowering the value of your money, what's actually going on is that *you're paying money to have money borrowed from you.*

Even mafia loan sharks don't try to go this far.

Near-0 percent, 0 percent, and negative interest rates hurt the innocent most—like our moms and dads. There they are laboring away for thirty or forty years, scrimping and scraping by, dropping coins in the "swear jar," setting a little bit of the paycheck aside every week, and putting their meager savings in the safest possible place—the credit union, the bank, U.S. savings bonds.

Current yield on a Series EE savings bond? 0.1 percent. Mom and dad would be better off tying up their rainy-day money in a sock. Yes, they might get burglarized. But you can shoot a burglar. It's illegal to shoot a governor of the Federal Reserve Bank.

What happens to mom and dad? They are forced to seek riskier investments in order get any return at all.

There's nothing necessarily wrong with *us* doing that. But it's wrong to make mom and dad do it. They are the children of hardship and wartime. They've seen all the risk they need to see.

Mom and dad are risk-averse. Thank God. That's why we're still alive. It was dad who nixed my plan to ski down Death Gulch on a pair of two-by-fours duct-taped to my galoshes.

Mom stopped me from jumping out the attic window with a pillowcase parachute onto an old couch cushion on the driveway. And mom and dad, acting quickly and in unison, prevented my attempt to use fifty cherry bombs to launch a coffee can into orbit.

Risk isn't right for mom and dad. It makes them feel guilty and uncomfortable. It's like serving roast beef to the parish priest during Lent.

Inflation is immoral, too. We who are moderately sophisticated about finances are savvy about the varying value of money. We can formulate investment strategies to offset the dire effects of inflation, maybe even to benefit from them.

But what about poor people? Their only available investment strategy is to invest what little money they have in food and shelter. Inflation is brutal on the poor.

If you were walking through a poor neighborhood and saw a little girl with an ice cream cone, you wouldn't take it away from her. I'd hope government wouldn't take it away either. But somehow, government thinks it's all right to bring the blow-dryer of quantitative easing into that poor neighborhood and stand over the little girl with the hot stream of air from the dryer pointed at her ice cream cone until it melts away to nothing.

That's a bad thing to do. And flooding the market with free capital is maybe even worse.

Free capital allows the marketplace to be swamped with business jerks. Some are incompetent. Some are corrupt. Many are both. Again, this isn't a problem for us. We're smart; we're well-informed. But what about people who aren't as lucky as we are?

Free capital hurts the frail and the weak. It is they who will be cheated by shoddy products and services and quack investment pitches. We shouldn't blame them for being cheated.

Maybe they suffer from intellectual disability. What with the state of our public school systems in America, there's a lot of intellectual disability going around.

The people who are harmed most by free capital are people who are operating at a disadvantage. Being kind to the disadvantaged is a core principle of morality.

You wouldn't trip a blind man. But, somehow, government thinks it's all right to go to the neighborhood where the blind man lives and take all the sewer grates off the storm sewers and all the manhole covers off the manholes.

That's an evil thing to do.

Next time you see someone who's in charge of Central Bank policy, take a close look at his pants cuffs or her open-toe kitten heels. Is what you see a cloven hoof?

# Debt Jubilee

When Satan is working on the economy, cheap money and the interest-free debt it creates are only two of the items in his toolbox. A much bigger wrench is debt abolition.

Individuals, private businesses, corporations, countries, continents, and the whole damn world are now so overburdened with debt that we could be facing a "Debt Jubilee"—a rare and dramatic event where some or much or most or even all debt is canceled.

For example, America's household debt. A financial analyst friend of mine wrote the following about American household debt.

> In the late 1980s, the 20% of Americans with the least income held little debt, when measured against their income levels. The poorest Americans now hold debts in excess of 250% of their incomes, or about five times more debt, proportionately, than the wealthiest 20%.
>
> This massive change in the character of our household debts came about because of "innovations" in lending—subprime auto loans, payday lenders, and student loans. Today total household debt is almost

$13 trillion, higher than the previous record of $12.6 trillion set just before the Great Recession.

My friend pointed out that when debt-holding becomes so grossly distorted the problem ceases to be financial and becomes sociopolitical. And that the sociopolitical actions can be chaotic, as the abandonment of the gold standard was, or even revolutionary, like the Soviet repudiation of Russian debt in 1917.

(My friend is a very pessimistic person.)

Debt Jubilee does indeed have a sociopolitical origin. Or, anyway, a sociopolitical-religious background.

The concept of a Jubilee has its basis in the book of Leviticus, Chapter 25. The Israelites were instructed that every half century there should be a reversion of land to its original owners or their heirs, a general forgiveness of debt, and a manumission of bond servants.

## Leviticus 25:13

*In the year of this jubilee ye shall return every man unto his possession.*

The slate is wiped clean and everybody gets to start over. It's a nice idea. (Never mind that *The New Oxford Annotated Bible* contains the following footnote: ". . . there is no evidence that the jubilee program was ever carried out . . .")

At one time or another most of us have wished for a Jubilee (involving both our financial and *personal* affairs).

But the imposition of a large-scale Jubilee on a credit-integrated, globalized twenty-first-century economy would be a disaster.

And I don't want that disaster to be blamed on ancient tribes of wandering Israelites whose Holy Torah was committed to writing early in the first millennium B.C., and in which events that took place a thousand years before were being recounted.

Things have changed since then.

Of course, *right* and *wrong* haven't changed. The Ten Commandments remain carved in stone just the way they were in the movie of the same name starring Charlton Heston.

But social rules and religious observances do change. For example . . .

### Leviticus 1:5

*And he shall kill the bullock before the Lord: and the priests . . . shall bring the blood, and sprinkle the blood round about upon the altar . . .*

O'Rourke though I may be, I've been to temple for Bar Mitzvahs and Bat Mitzvahs and have never seen anything like that.

Plenty of things are extant in the Bible that today's observant Jews and pious Christians frown upon—slavery, polygamy, child marriage.

God gives us rules according to time and circumstances. God does not speak through Moses to tell the ancient tribes of wandering Israelites, "Thou shalt not look upon thy iPhone at the dinner table."

The Jubilee—from the Hebrew word *yobel*, "ram"; hence, "triumphant blast of a ram's horn"—has its basis in the particular circumstances of the Israelites in the second millennium B.C.

The most important circumstance was that the Israelites lived in a zero-sum economy. They were farmers and shepherds. They were dependent on land. There was (with the exception of a brief parting of the Red Sea) a fixed amount of land. Land in the possession of someone else was land you couldn't plant or graze. And, if all the land was in the possession of someone else, you and your family starved.

Many primitive agriculturalists make some sort of provision for equal access to land. Julius Caesar, in *The Gallic Wars*, mentions that among certain German tribes it was not "permissible to remain dwelling in one place for more than a year."

The zero-sum nature of land is the opposite of the modern economy, where we can make more of everything. We can, in effect, make more land by vastly increasing the agricultural productivity of farms and fields. We can, in actuality, make more land by piling up the landings in skyscrapers.

Worthy of note in Leviticus, Chapter 25, is an exception to the Jubilee redistribution of land.

## Leviticus 25:30

> . . . *the house that is in the walled city shall be established forever to him that bought it throughout his generations; it shall not go out in the jubilee.*

People with their home in a walled city are presumably not farmers or shepherds. They're making a living from services, crafts, and trade.

Services, crafts, and trade are not—and never were, not even back when Moses was floating down the Nile in his baby basket—zero-sum endeavors.

The other circumstance that the Israelites faced was predatory lending. I'm talking about something much worse than payday loans. With payday loans there is, at least, a payday. This isn't always so among primitive agriculturalists.

The crops and herds of the second millennium B.C. were hit-or-miss. One too many lions lying down with your lambs and you could be wiped out. The Land of Milk and Honey may have been, climatically, a little sweeter and milkier than it is today, but it was still grievously drought-prone.

Farming is by nature credit-dependent. Income arrives but once a year. Sometimes it's bounteous and can hold you through the next harvest. Sometimes it's nil and when planting time comes you've eaten your seed corn.

The predatory lenders of the time were like the Mafia loan sharks of today. They had no commercial interest in you getting out of debt. They wanted the "vigorish," they wanted the "juice." (Literally, if you were growing grapes or olives.) Worse, they wanted you to *fail* to pay the vig, so they could move in on your business.

These were coercive loans. When you ran out of resources to repay you'd have to "lease" your land to the lender. When you ran out of land to lease you'd have to lease yourself and become the lender's bond servant.

The same thing is going on in rural India to this day . . . and in plenty of other dark corners of the globe.

But here and now, in the developed world's sophisticated conduct of business, industry, and commerce under the rule of law and the light of transparency, there should be no need for a Jubilee.

And yet . . . And yet . . .

Maybe, when we're pondering "Jubilee," we should be considering how many of the probably-never-to-be-paid debts that modern people have incurred are, in fact, the result of predatory and coercive lending practices.

There are, after all, other kinds of predation than the strictly financial. And there are other kinds of coercion besides brute force.

What about politically predatory loans made by government agencies looking to score populist points by luring poor people into impossible mortgage debt and suckering the young into gigantic student loans?

What about strategically coercive loans made by rich nations to poor nations to keep those poor nations in thrall?

What about World Bank and International Monetary Fund loans made for the sake of "political stability" that result in keeping predatory and coercive dictators in power?

A Jubilee in the biblical sense might not be the best basis for action. But the moral ideas that underlie the Jubilee remain a good basis for thought.

Among those thoughts is that we are only temporary visitors to the earth and our job is to take care of it in the short term and make it fruitful but also avoid permanently ruining the place . . . not only for our own sake but for the sake of the posterity that we'll never meet.

## Leviticus 25:23

*The land shall not be sold for ever: for the land is mine; for ye are strangers and sojourners with me.*

# SECTION III

## Mutant Capitalism

*Glendower:* I can call spirits from the vasty deep.
*Hotspur:* Why, so can I, or so can any man; But
will they come?

—William Shakespeare, *King Henry IV, Part I*

# Introduction

## *The Mutants*

If you don't know what I'm talking about, take a look at these two lists:

| The 12 Largest U.S. Corporations by Market Capitalization 2017 | The 12 Largest U.S Corporations Corporations by Market Capitalization 1987 |
|---|---|
| Apple | General Motors |
| Alphabet (Google) | Exxon |
| Microsoft | Ford |
| Amazon.com | IBM |
| Facebook | Mobil |
| Berkshire Hathaway | General Electric |
| Johnson & Johnson | AT&T |
| Exxon Mobil | Texaco |
| JPMorgan Chase | DuPont |
| Wells Fargo | Chevron |
| Bank of America | Chrysler |
| General Electric | Altria (Philip Morris) |

Capitalism has undergone a transmogrification. Much of capitalism has become unrecognizable. When I see the 1987 Top 12 list, I can tell you what every one of those companies did. Today I'm utterly ignorant about what seven of the Top 12 companies do.

Not only am I confused by the purpose of these corporations, I'm also perplexed by how—and, indeed, if—they make a measurable profit. Plus I'm dumbfounded by the way they're priced on the stock market. Thirty years ago it was simple: GM, Ford, and Chrysler made the cars. Exxon, Mobil, Texaco, and Chevron pumped the gas to make the cars go. Where the cars went was shopping. GE manufactured the things you went shopping for—washers, dryers, stoves, toaster ovens, locomotives, jet engines, etc. At work you used IBM stuff. They had typewriters you could pound on in a way that would send a modern touch screen straight to the Mumbai e-waste disposal. They had real computers, too, not these little flimsy silicon chip-dip kind, but big manly computers that took up whole rooms, spewed out punch cards, and helped put an American on the moon. While you were smoking a Marlboro you called home on an AT&T phone that you never lost because it weighed as much as a boat anchor, and you couldn't accidentally drop it in the toilet because the cord wouldn't reach that far. DuPont made the glue that held it all together and also lots of other chemicals, back when "Better Living Through Chemistry" was still considered a good idea.

Now . . . it's as if somebody took corporations and exposed them to atomic-bomb test radiation in a cheap Japanese science fiction movie and out sprang Godzilla, Mothra, and Rodan—or, as investors call them, Amazon, Facebook, and Google.

Thirty years is a very brief period in terms of economic evolution. For example, from the fall of the Roman Empire in 476 A.D. until the increased crop yields and trade of the 1400s, there was none. Industrialization supposedly happened at blinding speed but in fact took two hundred years to reach the far corners of the globe. I am frightened of scary mutants.

The mutants fall into four categories:

### The Bafflers

As far as I'm concerned, what Apple, Google, and especially Facebook sell are annoyance, noise, and distraction. I've got kids and dogs. Annoyance, noise, and distraction are unlimited free goods at my house.

I don't want to see photos of the adorable grandchildren of everyone I've ever met and videos of the cute things their cats do. Even less do I want to hear about the world's dullest experiences and most banal thoughts—which people save up for their Facebook postings. If Facebook wants to make money from me, I'll pay the website handsomely to go the hell away.

Google is a very handy device for getting facts. If you don't mind the facts being wrong. I'm a journalist, so I'm in constant need of wrong facts and therefore use Google all the time. So it's good for *me*. But how good it is for *you*, a reader of journalism, is another question.

Google has caused my research skills to degenerate to the point where I have to sing the kindergarten "ABC Song" to use the dictionary. Google is like the worst librarian in the world. You ask her a question and she says, "Well, there's a big pile of books over there, but we haven't gotten around to sorting them. However, we do have a tattooed skinhead and a Bernie supporter with a braided beard and a pink pussy hat in the reading room and you could ask them."

Then there's Apple, with its darned iPhone. I hate talking on the telephone. I consider being unable to come to the phone to be one of life's greatest luxuries. The last thing I want is a telephone that fits in my pocket, can find me wherever I go, fills my head with things like Trump tweets, curling tournament scores, and how I didn't win the lottery again, and calls me a cab because my wife says I should quit drinking and get home *right now*.

I want a phone the size of a cement block, like AT&T used to make, and I want it connected to an answering machine that says I can't come to the phone.

## The WTFs

I understand—sort of—why Microsoft is successful. It makes the most popular desktop computer operating system. What I don't understand is how to make that operating system quit operating. Every time I click my mouse I am confronted with a Rube Goldberg cartoon.

A computer is a fundamentally simple device—a combination IBM Selectric, filing cabinet, post office, and pocket calculator. But if I make one wrong move on my computer the filing cabinet mails me the Selectric, and the mailman drops the package on my desk and smashes the pocket calculator.

There is no excuse for the complexity of the Microsoft operating system. I picture a room the size of Redmond, Washington, full of pear-shaped e-nerds adding "features" because . . . because they can. I want to lock each of them in the garage with an IBM Selectric, a filing cabinet, a mail slot, and a pocket calculator and not let them out until my computer is as simple to use as my automatic garage door opener.

There is also no excuse for Microsoft making the most popular desktop computer operating system and then punting the mobile device operating system ball to Google's Android OS on first down in the mobile device game.

Why is Microsoft considered a blue-chip stock?

JP Morgan Chase, Wells Fargo, and Bank of America are three more WTFs. Not because of the companies themselves or their fundamentals (low price/earnings ratios and some dividend yield). But I have my doubts about whether banks should be among the American corporations with the highest market capitalizations. In fact, I have my doubts about whether banks should be publically traded corporations at all—instead of being partnerships.

Before 1970, the New York Stock Exchange banned banks from being publicly listed. Maybe the NYSE was right the first time.

All corporations face what's known as the "agency problem." The goals and interests of management can conflict with the goals and interests of proprietors.

It's a familiar enough problem. It happens around the house. Let's say I have a teenage daughter. (And I do. But she's remarkably well-behaved. Either that or she's incredibly discreet. Anyway, I'm not using her as an example. I'm using a *hypothetical* teenage daughter.)

My hypothetical teenage daughter is at an age where she insists that she can manage her own life. Her goal is to have a good time. Her interests are clothes, boys, and loud music with obscene lyrics.

Being a dad, I feel a proprietary interest in my daughter. My goal is to get her through college, settled in her career, and, eventually, happily married with adorable grandchildren whose pictures I can post on Facebook. My other interests are not paying for too many of her clothes with my credit card, letting the boys know I have a shotgun, and getting my daughter to turn down her mobile device so that I can't hear the obscene lyrics leaking out her earbuds.

Bankers, as we learned during the 2008 financial crisis, can be every bit as bad as hypothetical teenage daughters—except they weren't being hypothetical, they were going broke.

For all sorts of reasons (pay, perks, ego, stock option greed) the senior managers of banks got themselves involved in financial transactions no ordinary stockholder could understand—and, as it turned out, no senior manager could understand either.

Because the banks were owned by clueless stockholders, the banks' clueless senior managers were allowed to forget what banks are supposed to do—move money around in a safe and wise manner, taking a little cut for their trouble.

Then there are two WTFs who aren't answering attempts to contact them and determine what their mission is. "Earth to General Electric . . ." "Earth to Berkshire Hathaway . . ."

Google "General Electric" and this comes up:

GE | The Digital Industrial Company | Imagination at Work

Explore GE imagination at work. Learn how GE innovation builds, powers, moves & cures the world. We're changing the world one idea at a time.

More results from ge.com»

General Electric (@generalelectric) · Twitter

https://twitter.com/generalelectric

A 3D printed backpack lets engineers "steer" DragonflEye, a dragonfly cyborg drone, the smallest in the world. invent. ge/2tnwbAWpic.twitter.com/EpTfg1P . . .

1 hour ago • Twitter

3D printing shaved years off the production of a heart sta-
bilizer used in open heart surgeries. invent.ge/2vaWTKupic.
twitter.com/MZOanm3 . . .

1 day ago • Twitter

A massive @GEenergyConnect energy converter in the
North Sea will connect offshore wind energy to the land.
invent.ge/2unO2rN

5 days ago • Twitter

What does all that even mean? Well, out in the Midwest
where I come from, the last Tweet from GE would mean,
"Hurry up, Maw, get down in the root cellar. There's a twister
a-comin'!"

"Builds, powers, moves & cures the world"? According to
this description, GE produces an accretion of dust and gas in
the early solar system 4.6 billion years ago, then asks, "Did the
earth move for you too?" And when our planet suffers from
climate ills we're supposed to call GE CEO Jeff Immelt—who
got fired—and he'll tell us, "Take two asteroids and call me
in the morning." As for "powers . . . the world," I guess we're
supposed to think that the sun shines out of GE's . . .

How is a retail investor supposed to think anything co-
gent about this kind of company? And I'm not even touching
on GE's almost innumerable subsidiaries such as GE Capital
(which GE is trying like hell to get rid of); GE Automation
& Controls; GE Wind Energy, to make us less dependent on
petroleum; Baker Hughes oil field services to make us more
dependent on it; GE Jenbacher, which manufactures "cogenera-
tion modules," whatever those may be; and Amersham, with
its "radioactive material for peacetime uses." (Got a termite
problem? Contact Bikini Atoll Pest Control.)

Berkshire Hathaway is even more of a dog's breakfast than
GE, if a more successful one.

I count sixty-four companies controlled by Berkshire Hathaway, but it's early in the day and the number may have gone up by now.

Except for a group of insurance providers, most of the businesses the BRK-A companies are in bear a chalk-to-cheese relationship to the businesses the other BRK-A companies are in.

Here are just ten of them:

> NetJets
>
> *Omaha World-Herald*
>
> Acme Brick
>
> Fruit of the Loom
>
> Borsheims Fine Jewelry
>
> GEICO
>
> Burlington Northern Santa Fe Railway
>
> Dairy Queen
>
> Benjamin Moore
>
> Duracell

There's a story in there somewhere . . .

"Hop on a G3 and get here quick because—stop the presses—I'm marrying a brick. Need some new underwear. Already have the ring. The little lizard was going to be my best man, but he got run over by a train. We'll serve ice cream cones at the reception, then go out and paint the town red. It will recharge your batteries!"

But what's the story for the retail investor? It would take a genius to keep track of all this different stuff. Maybe Warren Buffett is a genius. But he's an eighty-eight-year-old genius. Think he remembers everything he's bought?

## The Price Puzzlers

Amazon.com, which is basically a glorified yard sale, doesn't pay a dividend, had a net income return of .5 percent on its market capitalization, and has a price/earnings ratio of 192.

Meanwhile Apple, which is considered to be a legendarily brilliant and innovative company, does pay a dividend, had a 6 percent net income return, and has a P/E of 17.6.

What's happening here is far beyond the brainpower of an old liberal arts major like me. But I'm told Apple's stock price is low because gigantic investment funds already own so much Apple stock that they can't stay diversified unless they buy something else.

That might cause a more conspiracy-minded person than myself to wonder how much freedom there really is in the "free market."

## The for-Profit Not-for-Profits

Four of America's top twelve companies—Amazon, Facebook, Google, and Berkshire Hathaway—don't pay dividends. All of them have net income. Even famed burner-through-capital Amazon had 2016 net income in excess of $2 billion, and Berkshire Hathaway had 2016 net income in excess of $24 billion. Not a penny of it went to shareholders.

I understand the idea behind plowing profits back into the business. There's a website called "The Balance" with a feature, "Investing for Beginners," that contains an essay on the subject using your dad and uncle's apple orchard as an example.

My dad and my uncle didn't sell apples, they sold cars. Plow your profits back into that business and you're buying the cars you just sold.

Buying a stock *only* because I expect someone else to buy the stock later for a higher price makes me feel like I've been reading a certain F. Scott Fitzgerald novel and rooting for Jay Gatsby.

Never taking a profit from a healthy business also reminds me—more than slightly—of my supposed savings account when I was a kid. Every Christmas and birthday a $5 bill and all of what I was paid for mowing the neighbor's lawn went right in there. The balance was several hundred dollars. "We're saving for your college education," my mother would say.

Maybe *we* were saving for my college education. But *I* was saving for a Wham-O slingshot. I had $2.38 in an old Prince Albert can, mostly from pop bottle deposits and change found under the sofa cushions. To this day I believe I would have been happier with taking one less English Lit course and shooting a lot more squirrels and pigeons. And I could have done it if Mom had at least let me collect my savings account interest payments.

Furthermore, Jeff Bezos, Mark Zuckerberg, Larry Page, Sergey Brin, and Warren Buffett don't seem to care about money as much as I do. Too much trouble counting it, probably.

Warren Buffett lives very modestly and has promised to leave all his money to charity. I have more respect and affection for money than that. I care.

Would you let somebody who didn't care about kids take care of your kids? Allow them to jump off roofs, tease vicious dogs, and stick silverware into electric outlets? I rest my case.

### Fighting the Mutants

Thankfully there are a couple of old-school holdovers in the Top 12. Exxon Mobil is standing by to wash your windshield and check your oil or, actually, these days, feed you fatty snacks at the gas station convenience store.

XOM's P/E is a noninsane 33.7 and its dividend yield is a fat 3.8 percent. Not bad for the middle of an oil bust.

Oil prices may never again reach a peak like 1979 when the sweater-wearing peanut farmer with the thermostat set to 60 was in the Oval Office. Or a peak like 2008 when China's tiger and India's . . . sacred cow, I guess . . . were first unleashed. But given what a cost/benefit flop "alternative energy" has been, it will be a long time before Exxon gas stations are selling bottled water for more than unleaded premium.

Johnson & Johnson, the pharmaceutical, medical device, and personal care products company, seems fairly priced at a P/E of 22.6 with a 2.5 percent dividend yield. The current Dow Jones Average P/E is 21.00 and the average dividend yield is 2.52 percent.

J&J makes baby powder, Band-Aids, and Tylenol. People aren't going to stop having kids. Kids aren't going to stop having skinned knees. And there are going to be some *big* headaches if the most bizarre of the Mutants—Amazon.com, 192 P/E, 0 percent dividend yield—go the way of Godzilla in *Godzilla, King of the Monsters!* (1954). Spoiler alert: Dr. Serizawa's Oxygen Destroyer.

We'd better get Dr. Serizawa back to work.

Mutant Capitalism is terrifying. But fortunately what's *immutable* is capital itself. Capital is the accumulation of wealth (of any kind, including skill and knowledge) to be used for producing more wealth.

We don't blow all our money, time, and smarts making whoopee. Instead, we deny ourselves a little bit of fun. We set aside (or we should set aside) some cash, some work hours, and some intelligence to make ourselves richer, more leisured, and increasingly savvy in the future.

This has been going on since cave people deliberately chipped extra flint spear points to trade with the cave next door for the smoked mammoth slices the neighbors intentionally didn't eat all of.

And this will continue to go on until we are taking our excess gray matter to the brain farm to grow an additional medulla oblongata to exchange with space aliens for the Whoopee Rays they didn't use up.

Capital*ism*, on the other hand, is the means by which capital is put to work. And capitalism is capable of taking some very strange forms.

For example, socialism, communism, fascism, and crony capitalism are all types of capitalism. The difference being that, unlike free market capitalism, the capital isn't primarily held by private parties and/or isn't put to work according to market principles of supply and demand.

With socialism the capital is held by dopey, dreamy, featherhead political and bureaucratic know-it-alls who are—occasionally—well-meaning but who are always self-serving.

With communism the capital is held by murderous totalitarian thugs.

With fascism, you get the same thugs plus the businesspeople who have brown-shirt-nosed them.

With crony capitalism, you hold the capital but you'd better do what Putin or the Saudi royal family or Bill and Hillary Clinton tell you to do with it.

We've survived the pinkos, the Reds, the Nazis, and (I hope) Bill and Hillary. If we keep a level head and put our common sense Oxygen Destroyer to work sucking the air out of the monsters, we'll survive Mutant Capitalism too.

# One Good Thing About Mutant Capitalists: They Aren't Playing Monopoly

Mutant Capitalism has a lot of worrying features. Let's not worry about the wrong ones. In particular let's not worry about whether these companies are "monopolistic."

The threat of monopoly in capitalistic commerce, industry, and finance has been a perennial bugbear for politicians, social critics, and do-gooders.

Maybe this is because warnings against monopolies go all the way back to the man who originally described how capitalism works. Adam Smith said in *The Wealth of Nations*, "The price of monopoly is upon every occasion the highest which can be got. The natural price, or price of free competition . . . is the lowest which can be taken."

More likely monopoly is a bugbear for do-gooders because the do-gooders are still mad about playing Monopoly with the smart kid from down the block (now running a hedge fund) who talked the do-gooders into letting him finance hotels on their Baltic and Mediterranean in return for giving him their Park Place to go with his Boardwalk.

Never mind that in a free market system monopolies are only possible with the bureaucratic enforcement powers of government. And government bureaucracy is controlled by politicians, social critics, and do-gooders.

Yet the five largest U.S. corporations, measured by market capitalization, *do* seem somewhat monopolistic on first impression:

Apple
Google
Microsoft
Amazon
Facebook

And first impressions matter.

In 1998 the Justice Department tried to break up Microsoft, accusing the company of engaging in anticompetitive practices in violation of the 1890 Sherman Antitrust Act. To put that in layman's terms, Microsoft was guilty of being too good at what it did.

Microsoft got there first with the best of the computer operating systems. But I doubt that, when penning his antitrust bill, Senator John Sherman (1823–1900) was thinking about a funny magic lantern show contraption that would sit on your desk one day in the distant future.

Microsoft settled the suit in 2001 by addressing some legal complaints I don't understand with some concessions I don't understand either.

Microsoft survived in one piece, but I bet that cost a whole bunch of 1s and 0s with a dollar sign in front.

Political socially critical do-goodery is (as most things are) worse in Europe. In 2004 the EU fined Microsoft €899 million for its excellence, and in 2013 it fined Microsoft another €561 million for failing to get un-excellent enough.

In 2017 the EU fined Facebook €110 million for monopolistic policies (not, alas, for allowing Hillary Clinton to "share" her Wellesley College commencement speech).

And the EU fined Google €2.4 *billion* for, among other things, restricting third-party websites from posting ads from Google competitors on Google. What? Macy's buys a billboard and Gimbels gets to advertise on it?

Not that there is a Gimbels (or much of a Macy's) left anymore, due to Amazon's predatory monopolistic behavior.

*Which doesn't exist!*

Amazon's portion of total U.S. retail sales is 5 percent.

I repeat: 5 percent.

Let's compare that with a *real* monopoly—me. I'm a total monopoly at my house. (At least I hope so. The UPS man is very buff . . .) Anyway, I have complete monopolistic control over retail sales to the O'Rourke household. (That is, if you don't count my wife, my daughters, my son, the UPS man who keeps bringing stuff no one admits to ordering . . .) And do you know what my portion of those retail sales are?

Um, neither do I.

Let's give up on my stupid comparison and just declare, "Amazon is *not* a monopoly." (But I bet my portion of O'Rourke retail sales is still more than 5 percent. Although that's because my tractor broke . . .)

Amazon, Microsoft, Facebook, Google, and Apple all suffer from "The Kleenex Problem." Their names have become synonymous with certain kinds of products.

This is also true of some kindred (and in one case subsidiary) Mutant Capitalist companies such as Uber, Airbnb, Twitter, and YouTube.

People with minds too small to contain more than one name for anything (e.g. politicians) assume that all e-commerce, computer operating systems, social media, search engines, smart phones, strangers taking you for a ride, unknown persons in the guest bedroom, incoherent thoughts had in the middle of the night, and time-wasting blurry videos are the products of monopolistic enterprise.

A better name for it might be "The Zipper Problem." Kleenex actually does have 47 percent of the U.S. nose-blowing market. "Zipper" was never even a corporation. The word was briefly trademarked by B. F. Goodrich in the 1920s, but only for use on rubber galoshes.

Until I looked it up I had a vague idea that there was an enormous "Zipper Inc." out there somewhere and that if it ever got greedy and decided to charge $10 per interlocking tooth we'd all be going around with our barn doors open and our dresses falling off.

Apple has only 18 percent of the global smartphone market and would have less if a certain competitor hadn't added the "liar, liar, pants on fire" feature to the Samsung Note 7.

Also, on a personal note, the Apple iPhone design reminds me of the featureless black monoliths that keep showing up and causing trouble in Stanley Kubrick's *2001: A Space Odyssey*. (Yes, my children are threatening to get me a Jitterbug for Christmas.)

Microsoft might have once had a monopolistic air about it, but Windows is no longer the leading, let alone the only, computer operating system. Google's Android has 40 percent of the market versus 36 percent for Windows.

This makes Microsoft and Google into what economists call an "oligopoly." Meaning there are so few sellers of something that the few can control the price that the many (the buyers) pay.

However, you can't have too much control over the price of your product when you've got competitors, like Linux, who are giving the product away for free.

Albeit, Linux is free in the sense that you've got to be living for free in your mother's basement and have unlimited free time to install it because you're unemployed. But, still . . .

Twitter, for all the press it gets, has . . . (Mr. President, Twitter founders Jack Dorsey, Noah Glass, Biz Stone, and Evan Williams send their warmest regards.) Twitter has a laughable 5.2 percent of the social media market.

Facebook does better with 39 percent. But tell my teenagers that Facebook has a monopoly on social media and they'll look at you as if you said the dog Googled "Spaniels In Heat" on PornHub.

To my children Facebook is about as interesting and hip as the school bulletin board. They have ways of electronically communicating with their peers that are so new, so devious, so incomprehensible to adults that, by comparison, the German Enigma machine was a secret decoder ring in a Cracker Jack box.

If Putin's famed group of computer hackers attempted to intercept messages about which boys are cute sent from my daughter Muffin to her best friend Bitsy, the hackers would end up running screaming from the Kremlin begging for jobs installing cable.

Only Google (79 percent of search engine views) and its subsidiary YouTube (78 percent of video sharing) have any monopoly bragging rights.

Getting a monopoly on video sharing is like getting a monopoly on stupid. I've known guys who tried. ("Hold my beer and watch this . . .")

As for Google, I've already described how awful it is as a search engine. This doesn't mean it won't remain dominant in the business for a while.

Maybe for a long while. Horses were dominant in the transportation business for thousands of years. Then one day it occurred to people that a horse is a thousand pounds of bad attitude that kicks and bites and stinks up the garage. And the horse went the way of the horse and buggy.

There's plenty to damn in the New Mutant Capitalism. But if you damn it for being monopolistic you're a horse's . . .

# What Are
# Corporations For?

Corporation—from the Latin *corporatus*, "having a tangible body."

Some corporations have great bodies. And some corporations should go to the gym.

But, either way, corporations are the basis of civilization.

A corporation is a group of people. The members of the group share the corporation's benefits but do not personally own the corporation's assets. Likewise, the members of the group are not personally responsible for the corporation's losses. They risk only what it cost them to become part of the corporation.

Actually, corporations *are* civilization.

If you were an ancient Roman citizen you were a member of the body of Romans, the *corporatus*. You got the benefits of high-flown rhetoric in the Forum, thrilling gladiator fights in the Colosseum, and Ben-Hur's exciting chariot race where Charlton Heston kills the bad guy in the Circus Maximus.

But you didn't actually own the Forum, Colosseum, and Circus Maximus. Which was a good thing because maintenance costs—such as washing Caesar bloodstains off the Senate floor and cleaning up after the lions ate the Christians—were high.

On the other hand, after the Fall of Rome, you didn't have to go out and personally repair the ruins of the Forum, the Colosseum, and the Circus Maximus. All you lost was what you'd risked by being part of the Roman Civilization corporate group—which was, unfortunately, your life. But you get my general point.

If you aren't civilized, you don't need a corporation. In fact, when you're an uncivilized hunter and gatherer, dragging a Forum, Colosseum, and Circus Maximus around with you is a bother.

But we are civilized. And we need not only the gigantic public corporation that is called the state, but also lots of smaller private corporations to raise capital for investment while limiting the risk of investing.

The basic asset/liability rules of for-profit incorporation were codified in Roman law more than 2000 years ago. And then conveniently forgotten.

Groups of free individuals banding together to give themselves access to extensive material resources just didn't go down well with the feudal lords riding around in their suits of armor lancing anybody who got in their way.

Free individuals could have hired Blackstone Security to blow holes through chain mail, gauntlets, greaves, and visors with HK416 assault rifles.

But for 14 centuries after the collapse of Roman civilization, "corporations"—when they existed at all—were merely trade guilds, royal grants of monopoly, or charters for town governments.

The modern corporation is surprisingly modern. You can read both Adam Smith's *Wealth of Nations* and Karl Marx's *Das Kapital* and see no mention of corporations in the sense of limited liability joint stock companies. Indeed you won't be seeing much at all, due to eyestrain, if you try to read both books in one day.

Real corporations don't come back into existence until the British Parliament's *Limited Liability Act of 1855* and *Joint Stock Company Act of 1856*. And corporations don't take their true contemporary form until the House of Lords decided the *Solomon v Solomon & Co. Ltd* case in 1896.

The *Solomon v Solomon* ruling confirmed that corporations are "legal persons." Otherwise corporations wouldn't have legal standing in court. You'd own shares in something that was imaginary—shares in flying ponies and candy-flavored rainbows. (Not that this can't happen anyway. For instance if you bought Snapchat stock.)

Corporations have property rights. Corporations can make binding contracts. Corporations can sue and be sued. Corporations can be convicted of serious crimes . . .

And here is where "legal person" does get a little silly. I guess a corporation can, metaphorically speaking, be strapped to the lethal injection gurney. But how do you put a corporation in jail?

During the General Motors bankruptcy of 2009 some of us would have liked to see GM sent to the slammer. But taxpayers would have had to build some enormous new federal correctional facilities to lock up GM's $82.29 billion in assets.

And then what would we have had? Thousands upon thousands of Cadillacs, Buicks, Chevys, Saturns, and Pontiacs rusting away in prison, rioting for better gasoline, and trying to get parole to sit on used car lots. (With the Pontiac Aztek in solitary for its own protection so that the other vehicles didn't beat it into scrap metal for having such ridiculous styling.)

But there is another, more serious, aspect to the "legal person" status of corporations. Corporations, as "legal people" turn out to have *personalities*, just like flesh and blood people do.

Corporations take on a life of their own. According to how corporations are managed, a corporation can be as likely as the next person to do you dirt. Or, as likely to be caring and sharing and benevolent.

When deciding to buy shares in a corporation, there's more to the decision than numbers on a spreadsheet. Especially if you're buying the shares as a long-term hold. You need to get to know the "legal person" that you're dealing with.

The purpose of a corporation—with its aggregation of resources, limited liability, and independent legal standing—is to watch your back. Make sure it's not back there picking your pocket.

# SECTION IV

## The Transition

Can we ring the bells backwards? Can we unlearn the arts that pretend to civilize, and then burn the world? There is a March of Science. But who shall beat the drums for its retreat?

—Charles Lamb, *Last Essays of Elia*

# Introduction

*The Digital Age and Which Digit It's Giving Us*

It is becoming, or has become already, a digital world. Which digit is it giving us? All of them—balled into two fists. We're going to be hit hard with a punch right in the privates.

A digital world does a lot of things, most of which I'm unenthusiastic about. But what I'm least enthusiastic about is the way a digital world enables a Security-and-Surveillance State.

We're on our way to a new life "Where Everybody Knows Your Name"—and your Social Security number, computer passwords, financial status, debit card PIN, credit rating, physical address, present whereabouts, etc.

Everything about us will be seen and known. And my greatest fear is that when we arrive in this place of universal visibility and ubiquitous public knowledge of all our thoughts and deeds, we'll *like it*.

A Security-and-Surveillance State that is all-seeing and all-knowing could replace religion. Something will. According to the Pew Research Center on Religion and Public Life, only about half of Americans age eighteen to twenty-nine are certain that they believe in any kind of God at all.

Central to the concept of God (or Gods) in every faith is that He (or They) knows (or know) exactly what we're up to at all times and why. This should be terrifying, but most people who are religious—myself included—seem more comforted than frightened by God's omniscience. Our original Security-and-Surveillance State was a state of grace—a oneness with God. Maybe a oneness with TSA will be just as good. Most Americans pass through airport security more often than they go to church.

Comfort with Security-and-Surveillance runs even deeper in the human psyche than religion. There's Mom.

She always knew what I was thinking. "Don't you even think about it," she'd say about the fresh-baked cookies before I'd caught a whiff of them. And she always knew what I was doing. She had eyes in the back of her head. Not only did she have eyes in the back of her head, she also had all the other eyes of all the other moms in the neighborhood. I'd come home from a jolly Saturday afternoon tormenting cats and tipping over birdbaths with my pals, and, before I was halfway up the front walk, I'd hear Mom: "No TV for a week!"

It hardly came as a shock when they taught us in Sunday school that "God is watching." Mom had gotten there before Him. Yes, God might—in some future too distant to be imagined—send us to hell. But He never smacked us on the butt with a wooden kitchen spoon. Much less did God wait until our fathers got home and tell them our sins so that we got a real whopping.

Plus we were also taught in Sunday school that "God is Love." And that He would "forgive us our trespasses," certainly including the foray into Mrs. Pulaski's yard where we cracked the head off her garden gnome with our Wham-O slingshots. And Mom, of course, was nothing but love. Can anything be as secure as a mother's love? Whatever we'd done, she got over it. Dad, too. By the time he'd had his second highball he'd forgotten all about giving us a real whopping and was out in the kitchen saying to Mom, "Boys will be boys . . ."

Then—to further muddle our attitudes about Security-and-Surveillance—there was Santa Claus.

> *You better watch out, you better not cry,*
> *You better not pout, I'm telling you why.*
> *Santa Claus is coming to town.*
>
> *He's making a list and checking it twice.*
> *He's gonna find out who's naughty and nice.*
> *Santa Claus is coming to town.*
>
> *He sees you when you're sleeping.*
> *He knows when you're awake.*
> *He knows if you've been bad or good,*
> *So be good for goodness' sake.*

And yet, after 364 days of my being a peevish brat, the Erector Set was under the Christmas tree anyway.

Due to our instincts and our formative experiences, it is all too easy to confuse a Security-and-Surveillance State with Mom, God, and Santa Claus.

The U.S. government *is* Santa Claus. Federal government annual per capita spending is $21,875. Everybody in America gets almost 22 grand apiece. Meanwhile what the average taxpayer gives to the federal government is only $9,655 a year.

Making up the difference must keep those elves at the North Pole busy.

The U.S. government is also Mom. There are a multitude of "eat your vegetables" federal laws on the books, all of them intended to make us healthy and safe, to give us "Security."

I'm not talking about what really gives us security. The Army, Navy, Air Force, and Marines go begging. (According to a DOD report, about 23,000 active-duty members of the armed services receive food stamps.)

I'm talking about things like the Occupational Safety and Health Act of 1970. The Act, as signed by President Nixon, was 39 pages of What's-Good-for-You that spawned a myriad of federal regulations and bureaucracies. A PDF of the Occupational Safety and Health Administration's "Field Safety and Health Manual" is 265 pages long.

Which is barely a note under a refrigerator magnet by federal What's-Good-for-You regulatory standards. The PDF for the U.S. Department of Heath and Human Service's Food and Drug Administration's Public Health Service "Food Code" is 768 pages long. "Don't put that in your mouth!"

The government has a vast apparatus to *secure* us. And an even vaster apparatus to *surveil* us.

It's not just the CIA, NSA, FBI, and Homeland Security. When it comes to U.S. intelligence and investigative agencies, their name is legion:

(I have printed the following list in very small type so that you won't read it all and experience a horrible fit of paranoia.)

Department of Agriculture Office of Inspector General U.S. Forest Service Law Enforcement and Investigations Department of Commerce Bureau of Industry and Security, Office of Export, Office of Security Enforcement, and Office of Inspector General National Institute of Standards and Technology Police National Oceanic and Atmospheric Administration and National Marine Fisheries Service Office for Law Enforcement Department of Defense Office of Inspector General, Defense Criminal Investigative Service, Pentagon Force Protection Agency, United States Pentagon Police, Department of Defense Police, Defense Logistics Agency Police, and Defense Intelligence Agency National Security Agency Police National Geospatial-Intelligence Agency Police Department of the Army Criminal Investigation Command, Military Police Corps, Counterintelligence, and Intelligence and Security Command Department of the Navy Naval Criminal Investigative Service, Marine Corps Criminal Investigation Division, Master-at-arms (United States Navy), Department of the Navy Police, Marine Corps Provost Marshal's Office, Marine Corps Civilian Police, Office of Naval Intelligence, and Marine Corps Intelligence Activity Department of the Air Force Office of Special Investigations, Security Forces, Air Force Police, and 25th Air force intelligence unit. Department of Education

Office of the Inspector General Department of Energy Office of Inspector General, Office of Health, Safety and Security, National Nuclear Security Administration, and Office of Secure Transportation Department of Health and Human Services United States Food and Drug Administration Office of Criminal Investigations National Institutes of Health Police Federal Protective Service United States Coast Guard Investigative Service and Coast Guard Police United States Customs and Border Protection Office of Air and Marine, Office of Border Patrol, and Office of Field Operations Federal Emergency Management Agency Weather Emergency Operations Center Police United States Immigration and Customs Enforcement Removal Operations United States Secret Service Transportation Security Administration Office of Law Enforcement and Federal Air Marshal Service Department of Housing and Urban Development Office of Inspector General and Protective Service Division Department of the Interior Bureau of Indian Affairs Police, Bureau of Land Management Rangers and Special Agents, Bureau of Reclamation Office of Law Enforcement, Hoover Dam Police National Park Service Division of Law Enforcement, Security and Emergency Services, United States Park Police, Office of Surface Mining Reclamation and Enforcement, United States Fish and Wildlife Service Office of Law Enforcement, and Division of Refuge Law Enforcement Department of Justice Bureau of Alcohol, Tobacco, Firearms, and Explosives, Drug Enforcement Administration, Federal Bureau of Prisons, and United States Marshals Service Department of Labor Office of Inspector General Department of State Bureau of Diplomatic Security and Bureau of intelligence and Research Department of Transportation Office of Inspector General, United States Merchant Marine Academy Department of Public Safety, and NHTSA Office of Odometer Fraud Investigation Department of the Treasury Bureau of Engraving and Printing Police, Financial Crimes Enforcement Network, Internal Revenue Service Criminal Investigation Division, United States Mint Police, and Treasury Inspector General for Tax Administration Department of Veterans Affairs Police Sergeant at Arms of the United States House of Representatives Sergeant at Arms of the United States Senate United States Capitol Police Library of Congress Office of the Inspector General Government Publishing Office Police Marshal of the United States Supreme Court United States Supreme Court Police Office of Probation and Pretrial Services United States Environmental Protection Agency Criminal Investigation Division National Aeronautics and Space Administration Office of Protective Services Office of Personnel Management Inspector General Federal Investigative Services National Background Investigations Bureau United States Postal Service Postal Inspection Service and U.S. Postal Police Smithsonian Institution Office of Protection Services National Zoological Park Police Amtrak Office of Security Strategy and Special Operations and Amtrak Police Federal Reserve System Federal Reserve Police and Federal Reserve Board Police Tennessee Valley Authority Police Nuclear Regulatory Commission Office of Inspector General National Science Foundation Office of the Inspector General National Archives and Records Administration Office of the Inspector General Railroad Retirement Board Office of Inspector General Small Business Administration Office of Inspector General Federal Deposit Insurance Corporation Office of Inspector General General Services Administration Office of Inspector General Social Security Administration Office of Inspector General United States Agency for International Development Office of Inspector General Corporation for National and Community Service Office of the Inspector General

But if the government wants to know our wickedest thoughts and most dastardly plans, none of this intelligence-gathering and investigation is necessary. We've posted those thoughts and plans on social media.

And if we've followed through on our stupidest ideas and put them into idiotic action, then we've got a video on YouTube with a million views.

Add our Social Media State to the Santa State and the Mommy State and we've already arrived at the Security-and-Surveillance State.

We *want* everyone to know everything about us. (And to take care of everything for us while they're at it.) Even the most secretive terrorists can't resist the opportunity to gurgle and coo—or bawl and wail—to attract attention.

The Security-and-Surveillance State makes us feel like we're the center of the universe again. It puts us back in the crib, without worry or responsibility. America used to need liberty and Fourth and Fifth Amendment privacy. Now America needs diapers.

# A Brief History of
# Economic Transitions

Every economic transition benefits the few. Only some economic transitions benefit the many.

We wouldn't want to do without economic progress, but
not every economic transition *is* progress.

The first major economic transition happened when the
economy was still very primitive. Two million years ago *Homo
erectus* came down from the trees and stood up on two legs.
(You can tell how primitive the economy was by the fact that
*Homo erectus* never licensed his name to any of the pharmaceutical companies who advertise to men on Fox News.)

Becoming bipeds was a splendid economic advance for
our ancestors, allowing them to walk to places where there
were good things to eat and run back with their arms full of
them. Unless they fell over. Which the members of the species
*Homo erectus* who *aren't* our ancestors did.

I'm guessing there was a "Pareto Distribution" among *Homo
erectus*. The Pareto Distribution (named after early twentieth-
century Italian economist Vilfredo Pareto) is a 20/80 split, a
commonly observed phenomenon in economics—20 percent
of workers do 80 percent of the work, 20 percent of clients
account for 80 percent of earning, 20 percent of investors

make 80 percent of the money, 20 percent of husbands help with the 80 percent of household chores done by wives, etc.

One out of five *Homo erectus* walked around looking for good things to eat. Four out of five grunted, "Standing up is too hard," or, "Standing up makes me dizzy," and sat back down. And were eaten by saber-toothed tigers.

At about the same time that we started to stand up we also started to make stone tools. The Paleolithic age was another major economic transition. Stone axes, stone knives, and stone spearheads allowed us to hit, stab, and spear things.

But, again, I'm guessing that paleo-technology baffled many cavemen. Try it yourself—make a sharp stone knife blade by taking one rock and knocking it against another. Having much luck? Me either.

If you and I had been around back then the things that got hit, stabbed, and speared would have been us.

The next important economic transformation was ten thousand years ago—the Neolithic Revolution, when agriculture began to replace hunting and gathering. This would seem to have been a win/win development for everyone concerned. You just sit there and watch the corn grow. Wheat, rye, and maize don't kick or bite or charge you with big horns. They can't run away. And they don't try to fool you when you're gathering them, the way delicious-looking deadly nightshade berries do.

But, as the prestigious British journal *New Scientist* says, "Decrease in physical stature and health in transition from hunter-gathering to agriculture is well-documented."

Turns out Neolithic farmers were smaller, weaker, less resistant to disease, and died a lot more.

Besides, where's the fun in sitting there watching the corn grow? Me for hunting some deer with my Remington .30-06 semiauto. We'll gather a few six-packs on the way home.

Slavery also caused an economic transition. And what a brilliant innovation slavery must have seemed. You used to have to work. Now somebody else has to work. And it's free. Well, almost free. You've got to provide some straw pallets and dole out thin gruel once a day and give the slaves an occasional break to drink out of a mud puddle.

Slavery was a brilliant innovation unless you were a slave. And that was fairly likely. Historians estimate that at the beginning of the Roman Empire, in the first-century B.C., between 35 percent and 40 percent of the people in Italy were slaves.

Free slave labor also didn't make things easier for the working-class Romans, the plebeians. The Imperial Minimum Wage was, basically, 0.

I suppose the plebs could have attempted to undercut that . . . "I'll bring my own straw pallet, bowl of thin gruel, and mud puddle." But . . .

When the Roman Empire fell and the Middle Ages came along, the plebeians were economically transitioned into serfs, villeins, and other forms of peasantry. This at least got them outdoors and into the fresh air, delving and spanning on the large manors of feudal barons.

Baronial manors were efficient economic institutions, at least compared with rapine and pillage, the other economic institutions of the era.

The medieval peasants, however, did not seem to have been very grateful for this economic efficiency. There were violent peasant uprisings in A.D. 841, 928, 1277, 1323, 1343, 1358, 1381, 1382, 1401, 1409, 1437, 1441, 1450, 1453, 1462, 1478, 1485, and 1498.

The only economic good news for ordinary people during the Middle Ages was the Black Death. It did have side effects in the 1340s and 1350s, killing between 30 percent and 60 percent of Europe's population. But consider the benefits:

upward pressure on wage rates and benefit packages resulting from supply-side labor market shortfalls.

The discovery of the New World meant a literal economic
transition. The Spanish transitioned an estimated $530 bil-
lion worth of silver and gold from the Western Hemisphere
to Europe on their treasure fleets.

There were only about 90 million Europeans at the time.
This meant that each of them got $5,888.88 apiece and every-
body was rich. Or so simple arithmetic would tell us.

Simple arithmetic would also tell us that the people who
lived in the New World lost $530 billion, and modern research
indicates that European diseases killed as many as 90 percent
of them. If you were a surviving Native American, you were
a rounding error. And broke, too.

But the Industrial Revolution was great for everyone . . .
everyone, that is, who was rich already. They were selling the
coal on their estates, making steam at their factories, and spinning cotton in their mills. We were mining the coal, shoveling
it into boilers, and working as child laborers on the looms.

Eventually, of course, the Industrial Revolution *was* great
for everyone. Microwave ovens for rich and poor alike!

And the scientific knowledge and technical expertise that
resulted from the Industrial Revolution led directly to the
Digital Revolution.

The Digital Revolution may be the most significant economic transition since we came down from the trees.

Will it benefit the few? Will it benefit the many?

We'll use me as an example of the many and Mark Zuckerberg as an example of the few. How have we been doing
—comparatively?

Let's start in 1987. That was when *Time* named the Personal Computer as its "Man of the Year." We'll count 1987 as
the beginning of the Digital Revolution.

In 1987 I was a freelance magazine writer with an uncertain income stream. I owned a little (mortgaged) house in the country. I had about $20,000 equity in the house and maybe $10,000 in the bank and an old pickup truck. My net worth was about $31,500.

In 1987 Mark Zuckerberg was three. I think we can fairly calculate his net worth (assuming a piggy bank) to have been in the low one figures.

The Digital Revolution has now been going on for thirty years.

I am a freelance magazine writer with an uncertain income stream. I own a large (mortgaged) house in the country. I have three children in private schools and an old pickup truck. My net worth (adjusted for inflation) is about $31,500.

Mark Zuckerberg's net worth is $72.3 billion.

# A Blockhead Confronts
# the Blockchain

Let us take crypto-currency as the ultimate (for the moment) manifestation of the transition to the Digital Age. Nothing is more fundamental to an economy than a medium of exchange. And our medium of exchange is doing its best to become incomprehensible to me.

People have all sorts of feelings about crypto-currency—wild enthusiasm, cool skepticism, greedy desire, utopian hope.

The feelings I have are ignorance and guilt. Let me try to explain the guilt.

I'm a libertarian, and I want a medium of exchange—a kind of money—that adheres to libertarian principles.

Actually, money that adheres to just one libertarian principle will suffice. This is the privacy principle: *"What I do that doesn't physically harm you is none of your \*&^%ing business."*

Business is conducted with money. Crypto-currency would seem to be the private kind of money libertarians want.

It's private in the two most important senses of privacy. First, crypto-currency is not public and therefore isn't subject to government public policy.

Government public policy with money is to issue as much money as the government feels like issuing.

Government treats money like a stalker treats posting things on your Facebook page. A couple of clicks of a Federal Reserve keyboard and there's another creepy rant. The original rant didn't have much value, and subsequent rantings are increasingly worthless and worrying. But unfriending the government is hard.

Second, crypto-currency encrypts transactions. What you're buying or selling isn't revealed to a nosy snoop. That nosy snoop being, once again, government.

I'm a pretty law-abiding guy. I'll wait for the "walk" light on an empty street corner in the middle of the night. I don't even cheat on my taxes—any more than federally mandated tax loopholes force me to.

I wouldn't use crypto-currency for any criminal scheme. (Well, except maybe to get Cuban cigars.) But no matter how legal the purchases I make are, I don't like those private purchases being on the public record in sales receipts and credit card records available to who-knows-which-nosy-snoop government agency.

And I don't like other people's purchases being on the public record either. If somebody buys a plastic inflatable anatomically correct Minnie Mouse doll for intimate relations in the privacy of his home, I sure don't want to know about it.

I don't want government to know about it either, for fear the EPA may impose endangered plastic rodent regulations on us all. Or maybe some high-minded EPA functionary will leak the information to PETA, causing the inflatable mouse doll store to be vandalized when my car is parked nearby within paint-tossing range.

I'm more worried about government abusing its police powers than I am about individuals abusing their purchasing powers.

My taking delivery of a thousand rounds of 9mm ammunition is information the government does not need to have.

No thank you to Homeland Security agents in body armor rappelling from helicopters into my backyard target range demanding an explanation for my blowing holes in a thousand empty beer cans. And they'd probably be accompanied by a Department of Health and Human Services counselor insisting I go into a treatment program for drinking a thousand cans of beer.

So that's the case in favor of crypto-currency. What makes me feel guilty (or feel like I should feel guilty) is that I don't support or advocate crypto-currency. I don't even find the idea of crypto-currency very interesting. In fact, I have no use for the stuff.

As of this writing, the market value of 1 bitcoin is about $16,000. But if you wanted to buy the banged-up Volvo station wagon that I got for my teenage kids to bang up some more and you offered me 1 bitcoin for it, I'd tell you to bite me.

This is because I feel ignorant. I am confused by the mathematical intricacies used to form the computer-programmed blockchains that underlie crypto-currencies.

Of course, I'm confused by lots of things. I'm confused by women, which didn't stop me from marrying a delightful one. I fly on airplanes all the time while having no idea why they take off or how they land.

But I am particularly sensitive to confusions concerning money. The history of money is a history of increasing confusion—much of it deliberate.

As I have previously flamed on the subject . . .

When the medium of exchange was barter, we were doing things like trading goats for pigs. Unless we were so stupid that we fell for the old "pig in a poke" trick, what we saw was what we got.

The move to "commodity money," with prices set in coins made of something valuable (gold, silver, copper), complicated trade. Yes, making change was easier. (No more having to pay for a goat by fishing a ham and three pork chops out of our pocket.) But it raised new questions. How to assay the metal content in coins? Who to trust to mint them?

The advent of "fiduciary money"—pieces of paper redeemable in coins—meant further confusions. Who really had those (possibly dodgy) coins? Where did they keep them all? Did they have enough?

And then came "fiat money." This is what government prints when it feels like it. Most of the money in the world today is fiat money. We've got it because government says we've got to.

No intrinsic value is involved in fiat money, just a pronouncement of existentialism from Central Banks. Trillions and trillions of dollars, euros, pounds, and renminbi are singing "We're Here Because We're Here Because We're Here Because We're Here." (A popular tune in the trenches during World War I—appropriately enough, since WWI was when fiat money came into global use.)

By now anybody who isn't confused by currency is simply insane. And the extra confusions of crypto-currency aren't the antipsychotic medication that's needed.

Crypto-currency even adds a kind of unwelcome mysticism to the already baffling material and philosophical aspects of money. Some regard the blockchain with almost religious awe, as if it were the work of mythical "Geek Gods" high upon Mount Laptopus.

An article by Marco Iansiti and Karim R. Lakhani in the January–February 2017 issue of the *Harvard Business Review* claimed that blockchain technology "has the potential to create new foundations for our economic and social systems."

No it doesn't.

I give you this from Wikipedia, where information was drawn from more extensive 2015 and 2016 articles in *The*

*Economist*, *Fortune*, and *Wired*: "A blockchain is a decentralized and distributed digital ledger . . . authenticated by mass collaboration powered by collective self-interests . . . This allows the participants to verify and audit transactions inexpensively."

One small step for man, one giant leap for accountants!

The blockchain is a tremendous, life-changing innovation —if you're a CPA. Throw those green eyeshades in the air! Dance around your spreadsheets with wild abandon!

Yes, the blockchain is confusing, but what it is, even more so, is boring.

However, it's also secret and secure.

I *don't* think.

There is the crypto-currency "blooper reel" to be considered:

In 2013 the Chinese bitcoin trading platform GBL suddenly shut down—a $5 million "bit*con*."

In 2014 the Mt. Gox bitcoin exchange declared bankruptcy after "losing" $473 million worth of customers' bitcoins. (Did Gox look under the couch cushions?)

In 2015 a crypto-currency called Paycoin was offered through something called "Customer Portal." In a Zen-like experience, ten thousand clients were left to meditate on being freed from the worldly burden of having $19 million.

In 2016 the founder of the Florida crypto-currency market Cryptsy was accused of misappropriating millions of dollars and then fleeing to China, perhaps to go to work for GBL.

And in 2017, $53 million in Ethereum crypto-currency disappeared from Ethereum's "Decentralized

Autonomous Organization," which turned out to be a little too decentralized and autonomous to qualify as being organized.

But let's chalk that up to experience. What's half a billion dollars among virtual friends? Every new technological development has its missteps. Such as the time Thomas Edison electrocuted Topsy the elephant to prove that AC electrical current is more dangerous than DC electrical current.

(Edison's actual involvement in frying Topsy may be—like the security of your crypto-currency account—dubious. But it's one of those stories—such as *Crypto-Currency Is the Money of the Future*—that we journalists call "too good to check.")

Crypto-currency on the World Wide Web does not create monetary security, or secrecy either.

Money has always involved insecurities and secrets. Banditry, after all, was invented long before cash was. When we were trading goats for pigs, it was hard to hide them under a mattress. They squeal and bleat. Bandits would steal the pork roast *and* the Libyan hamburger.

But you can shoot a bandit. You can shoot a computer, too, for all the good it will do in getting your goat back, which is why I stick to beer cans.

The Internet is an enormous hacking industry serviced by a small global interconnected computer network.

These hackers can hack *anything*. According to major news outlets, Russian hackers hacked into the American electoral system, right down to the level of presidential primary ballots.

I've been covering American elections since 1972, and I know absolutely nothing about what goes on behind the scenes with presidential primary ballots, and neither do all the political reporters I know. Talk about "encryption"—local politicians have primary voting shenanigans *sealed* in a crypt.

And yet here were the Russian hackers in Yoknapatawpha County, Mississippi—probably unable to understand a word of English as it is spoken by Mississippians—figuring out which yokel supporting Hillary would beat which hayseed supporting Bernie to become a Mississippi delegate to the Democratic National Convention.

And right now some dateless pear-shaped sixteen-year-old wearing emoji pajamas is in his bedroom with the floor covered in empty Snickers wrappers logging on to make himself a Darknet billionaire. I hope Walgreens accepts crypto-currency in payment for acne cream.

I have an old friend, Michael Farr, president of Farr, Miller & Washington investment consultants, who tells a story he calls "How Ignorance Saved Me a Fortune."

At the end of 2000, Enron was rated "most innovative large company in America" by *Fortune* magazine's "Most Admired Companies Survey." Michael thought it might be a good buy. He asked his top analysts to look at Enron.

A week went by and Michael heard nothing from his analysts. He talked to them and they said, "We're still working on it."

Another week went by. Nothing. "We're still working on it."

Two more weeks went by and Michael called his analysts on the carpet. He said, "A month ago I asked you to look at Enron. And I haven't heard a damn thing."

Michael's analysts said, "Do you remember what you told us when you hired us?"

Michael said, "Um . . . no."

"You told us," the analysts said, "that the first thing to do is figure out how a company makes money."

"And . . . ?" said Michael.

"We've been doing nothing but look at this company for the past four weeks, and we are still utterly ignorant about how Enron makes money."

Enron's 2001 bankruptcy cost investors more than $68 billion. Michael hadn't invested.

He says, "If I *hadn't* been ignorant, I'd be broke."

# What's the Connection?

Crypto-currency is dependent on computer connectivity. If we desire to put ourselves into various exotic positions with crypto-currency, we'd better first get a grasp on computer connectivity, or we'll be like . . .

A former chief economist for the New York Stock Exchange told me this joke: "An economist is a fellow who knows a thousand ways to make love and doesn't have a girlfriend."

Computers were an interesting invention, useful for such things as decoding secret messages when Nazis got Enigma machines and solving math problems such as, "If a train leaves Pittsburgh for Chicago going forty mph and another train leaves Chicago for Pittsburgh going fifty mph . . ." But, really, who cared? I wasn't headed to either Pittsburgh or Chicago.

For the first forty-some years of their existence, computers were mostly just a cross between a gigantic adding machine and a high-speed filing cabinet. They were hardly life-changing.

The most significant interaction with a computer that I remember from those days had to do with the computer punch cards used for college course registrations. Step on one of those with a golf shoe and you could find yourself assigned to a class in advanced astrophysics instead of "Rocks for Jocks."

The really interesting invention was connecting all those computers—the Internet.

Whether the Internet was a *good* invention . . . Well, no invention or innovation is intrinsically good or bad. When cavemen discovered fire the first thing they probably used it for was to cook—each other.

I go back and forth on the virtues of the Internet. Sometimes I am awed by my instantaneous access to enormous troves of important information. "What was the name of the child actor who played Jerry Mathers' pudgy best friend Larry on *Leave It to Beaver*?"

Other times I wonder, "Whose idea was it to put every idiot in the world in touch with every other idiot?"

Larry was played by Rusty Stevens.

The Internet presents a variety of problems, some inherent, some exogenous. And all of the problems pertain to questions about crypto-currencies.

The Internet is a vulnerable system. Its integrity cannot be assured. This is not because of genius hackers or careless users. The vulnerability is more a matter of the "Infinite Monkey Theorem." An infinite number of moneys hitting keys on keyboards for an infinite amount of time will inevitably write the complete works of Shakespeare, not to mention crack your password (name of first pet plus high school locker combination).

People connected to the Internet now number 3.2 billion, and estimates of how much time they spend on the Internet per day range as high as ten hours. Thus in just one "Infinite Monkey Year" you get 3.2 billion times 3,650, which may not equal infinity but is a big enough number to get the Infinite Monkey Theorem moving.

Then there's the vulnerable system behind the vulnerable system—the electrical grid upon which computer technology depends.

I understand something about electricity. I understand I often don't have any at my house.

I live in a remote part of New England, up a big hill, way out at the very end of the power line. And *anything* will cause my power to go out—ice, snow, wind, rain, autumn leaves, mating squirrels. You name it, and the O'Rourkes (and their computers) go dark.

I'm not blaming the electric company—even though the recorded message on their power outage hotline does say, "See you next summer!"

I understand the problems faced in creating a reliable electric grid.

And I understand the problems faced in generating electricity—because of all the time I spend trying to start my generator.

For some government regulatory reason I do not understand, the only gasoline I can get for my generator contains at least 10 percent ethanol. In minus-20-degree New England weather, the alcohol turns gasoline into a frozen daiquiri.

Giving daiquiris to my generator's little engine does not make it happy. Or, possibly, giving daiquiris to the little engine makes it *too* happy. Every time I yank the starter cord, I'm feeding the engine booze. Then it goes to sleep.

Besides the primary and secondary vulnerabilities of the Internet, there's the fact that the thing itself was created by people utterly ignorant of all free market principles. This is not conducive to best practices in the field of crypto-currency.

The Internet began as a collaboration between the military and academia—two institutions that are good at spending money but which have never turned a profit. In fact, their missions are to be perfectly unprofitable, by breaking things and killing people in one case and turning young minds to mush in the other.

True, a lot of commerce is conducted on the Internet, but it's a marketplace without fundamental market principles.

For forty-five years I was a writer. Now I'm a "content provider." And what's the foundational ethic of the Internet? "Content is free."

Which leads to an inherent triviality in what's on the Internet and also in how the Internet is operated. Planning to store a fortune on the Internet is not a trivial matter.

People do not take the Internet as seriously as they should.

With what excitement and anticipation did people once say, "There's a machine for that."

With what apathy and indifference do people now say, "There's an app for that."

Here are some of the things computer connectivity famously does: (And I'll leave out social media, because it doesn't seem to be very social and the noise-to-signal ratio disqualifies it as a medium of communication.)

- Google searches so filled with cinders and slag that looking for the factual is like sifting through the ashes of the Great Library of Alexandria.

- GPS giving us directions in the manner of a New Hampshire Yankee farmer leaning on a fence rail and chewing a blade of hay. "Go on down to where old Mavis Frick used to live and then turn right at the place where the barn burned down in 1958."

- Uber—if *Taxi Driver* gets remade it won't star Robert De Niro and Jodie Foster, it will star Elizabeth Warren in a driverless car.

- Driverless cars. What's next, eaterless meals?

- The means to binge-watch TV—which, speaking of eaterless meals, is as delightful as having the means to binge-eat *kale*.

- While wearing earbuds. They're a sort of reverse hearing aid that blocks out anything worth listening to. The Millennial Generation's motto is, "Huh?"

- Meanwhile the iPhone blocks your sight of anything worth looking at. Imagine a person from even fifteen years ago being told that what the future holds is humanity looking at its phone all day.

- Amazon has transformed shopping from a pleasurable excursion and happy social interaction into something more like going into the outhouse with a Sears catalogue to browse and use as Charmin.

- Internet comparison pricing also takes the sharp, eye-for-a-bargain intelligence out of shopping. But that's okay. We don't need real intelligence. We have artificial intelligence—everywhere.

My toaster has a brain. What a way to kick off a gloomy Monday morning—being outsmarted by a toaster.

Then, I work from home rather than an office. Instead of hanging out at the water cooler gossiping, flirting with coworkers, and making sports bets, I'm overwhelmed by big data flooding my personal communication devices.

And if I go somewhere else to work, I come home to a "smart house." It was bad enough when the house contained nothing but the kids getting smart with me. Now they've got the thermostat, the burglar alarm, and the toaster on their side.

To take an example of Internet triviality from my own field, the computer network is a handy device for writers. But does it improve the quality of what gets written?

When words had to be carved in stone, we got the Ten Commandments.

When we had to make our own ink and chase a goose around the yard to get a quill (and before the Infinite Monkey Theorem was developed), we got William Shakespeare.

When the fountain pen was invented, we got Henry James.

When the typewriter came along, we got Jack Kerouac.

And with the Internet we get—the President of the United States on Twitter.

When it comes to crypto-currency and computer connectivity, just be sure that "progress" doesn't do to your money what it's done to literature.

# What Has
# the Digital Revolution
# Done to Print Media?

*Killed It Dead*

Great literature is gone. Good journalism has disappeared. Philosophy dove off the high board of thought only to find that the pool of thinking had been drained. Even comic books have been ruined.

Let us consider Superman; his alter ego, Clark Kent; and Lois Lane, the woman who, unbeknownst to herself, loves them both.

*Superman* was created by Jerry Siegel and Joe Shuster in the mid-1930s, at the height of print media's influence.

For Superman to be at the scene and take action against villainy, it was natural to disguise him as mild-mannered newspaper reporter Clark Kent. That's what newspaper reporters did eighty years ago—be at the scene and take action against villainy (albeit with the power of the press rather than with being faster than a speeding bullet, more powerful than a locomotive, and able to leap tall buildings in a single bound).

What if *Superman* were created today? The *Daily Planet* is long out of business. Clark Kent and Lois Lane are bloggers.

They meet in a chat room but never see each other in the flesh ("ITF").

Sometimes Superman will "sext" Lois with pictures of himself posing in his blue pjs with his red underpants worn on the outside. And she'll reply, "LOL," because Superman has gotten very pudgy sitting at the computer all day. He's still living at home in Smallville, with his adoptive parents, the Kents. He has an apartment over the garage.

Due to computer hacking everybody knows that "Clark Kent" is Superman. Besides, there are no phone booths left for him to change clothes in, and Superman is too fat to fit into a phone booth anyway. And the only places where he *could* change clothes are monitored by security cameras.

Superman continues to believe in "Truth, Justice, and the American Way." But he's confused about which way to go with it. He gets all his news from wackadoodle websites, alt-right podcasts, and presidential tweets.

Therefore, when he flies off to fight villains ("Look! Up in the sky! It's a blimp . . . It's a hot air balloon . . . It's . . .") the villains often turn out to be imaginary.

Superman will come crashing through the ceiling of the MSNBC set for *Morning Joe* only to find that Joe Scarborough and Mika Brzezinski have pretaped the episode.

Of course, the villains in the original *Superman* were also imaginary—Lex Luthor and Mr. Mxyzptlk. But that was in a comic book.

Comic books are a medium for idiots. And so is the Internet.

Literacy is hard to attain. And we've quit trying.

Learning to read and write is very difficult. Homo sapiens evolved about 300,000 years ago, and for 295,000 years they never wrote anything down. Imagine the inconvenience of their grocery lists. Primitive man had to drag along gnawed mammoth bones, chewed cave bear fat, and the skulls of his enemies with their brains sucked out to remind him what to shop for. But even that was easier than writing a grocery list.

And when people did begin to write grocery lists, in Mesopotamia, in the fouth-century B.C., there was no one to read them. Literacy rates in civilizations where written communication was first developed are estimated to have been less than 1 percent.

You'd take your grocery list to the grocer and he'd say, "That's just a bunch of cuneiforms. We're out of cuneiforms. But the figs are nice."

Over the next five millennia things did not progress quickly. In 1550 Western Europe, the most advanced and developed part of the world, had a literacy rate of less than 20 percent. In 1950 the global literacy rate was still only about 56 percent. I have a copy of my great-grandfather O'Rourke's marriage certificate with an X where his signature should be.

Although maybe Great-Granddad had been drinking. People would rather drink than read and write. People would rather do *anything* than read and write.

People would rather thump on a tub, blow into a bottleneck, listen to a banjo, and sing ninety-six verses of "Old Stewball." Folk music is a perfect example of how desperate people are to entertain themselves by any means other than reading and writing.

Reading rubs us the wrong way because to be human is to be dyslexic. Which direction does what chicken scratch go? What squiggle sounds like which squawk? Have I got my hangers where my pothooks ought to be?

It's a problem we've had forever. Look at the ancient Greek alphabet: Γ, Λ, Ω, Ψ. The ancient Greeks had the "L," "V," and "U" upside down and the "E" sideways. No wonder nobody could read.

Reading is as hard as thinking, and people hate to read just as much as they hate to think. Never mind that reading and thinking are good for them.

The world would be spared a lot of trouble if people read and thought more. The invasion of Mogul hordes, for instance. What if Genghis Khan had thought it over and read up on the subject. He would have said, "Wait a minute . . . I'm invading Kazakhstan? For what? I think I'll just stay in the tent with my five hundred wives."

To read *is* to think. Higher thought is impossible without a means of transcription. How could Albert Einstein explain "$E = MC^2$" without writing it on a blackboard? He'd have to tell the physics class, "There's a stick sticking straight up with three more sticks pointing out of it this way. After that two flat lines, one on top of the other. Then a picture of a mountain range and a silhouette of a tit plus a mark that means two-of-something, but little bitty and up where the tit's shoulder would be."

With the spread of reading and writing, mankind's long journey up from mental darkness began.

From the middle of the nineteenth century to the middle of the twentieth century, there was a golden age of print media. People would read anything. People read *poems*. People read really, really long books. An empty ship bound for Australia could use the weight of one copy of an average George Eliot novel for ballast.

Big cities had so many different daily newspapers that there weren't enough plucky young newsboys shouting "Extra! Extra! Read All About It!" to sell them all. Sometimes the newspapers had to double up on the plucky young newsboys and have them shout, "Extra! Extra! Read All About It! Twice!"

Working men discussed James Joyce in pubs. One work-ingman would say to another, "Now yer *Finnegans Wake*, like, it goes takin' the form of discontinuous dream-narrative is wot oi sez." And the other workingman would reply, "Too right, mate. An' oi sez it blends yer English lexical items with yer neologistic multilingual puns."

True, early in that golden age people didn't always know good reading and writing from bad reading and writing. They'd get off on the wrong track and read *Das Kapital* or *Mein Kampf*. But by the 1950s everybody was reading *Peyton Place* and it seemed as if we were headed into a world of well-informed and clearly reasoning citizens. (Unless the commie Russians dropped the complete works of Dostoyevsky on us and we were all destroyed.)

Then the computer arrived and mankind's long journey up from mental darkness came to an abrupt halt.

Even in the 1960s era of punch cards, we'd quit looking things up in books and had started to "ask the computer." The computers of the day, of course, had very modest computational capacities and could only answer "0" or "1," but that was enough. You can see what computers did to our minds in the well-informed and clearly reasoned plan for a Vietnam War. Vietnam 1/USA 0.

Computers instantly reduced our attention spans to an instant. I know that for a fact. I Googled it.

Will something new and wonderful arise from the Digital Revolution to replace the masterpieces of print media?

We can hardly count ourselves human without the aesthetic and intellectual feelings brought forth by Shakespeare when he wrote . . .

> *To be, or not to be—that is the question:*
> *Whether 'tis nobler in the mind to suffer*
> *The slings and arrows of outrageous fortune,*
> *Or to take arms against a sea of troubles . . .*

Those feelings will always be with us. Except now they'll look like this:

# Five Lessons About the Digital Economy from a Member of the Digital Generation

I haven't seen my eldest daughter, age nineteen, face-to-face for years.

No, her mother and I aren't divorced. I didn't lose custody. My daughter and I aren't estranged. Her nose is buried in her iPhone. All I see is the top of her head.

Which gave me an idea. Like many people my age, I'm puzzled by the "digital economy." What parts of it will succeed? What parts will fail?

A Digital Generation has come of age, living in a digital world. This generation's tastes, preferences, and opinions will determine the fate of the digital economy.

They've already made some corporations, investors, and key players rich—and others broke. And that's just the beginning. The Digital Generation's peak earning years are yet to come. We'd all like to know what will happen when today's kids run tomorrow's economy.

And here I was with a one-girl focus group sitting right across the breakfast table, so deeply involved in the digital economy that her hair was dragging in her nut butter and chia seed toast.

All I had to do was get her attention. "Honey," I said, "I've hidden your car keys."

"WHERE?!" said my daughter.

"Inside a twenty-dollar bill," I said. "And I'm sure I can find them if you'll spend a few minutes letting me interview you about the digital economy."

"The *what* economy?" my daughter said. I tried to explain. She got an A in her high school econ class, but she looked at me like I was talking smack.

## Lesson #1
## When analyzing the digital economy, delete the word "digital."

People under twenty-one take the digital world so much for granted that "digital" isn't even a thing. This is because the Digital Revolution is over, and digital won. Everything we mean by "digital economy" has already been integrated into the economy itself.

## Lesson #2
## Put not your faith (or your money) in high-tech devices.

Me: "What are the various kinds of devices that you use to listen to music, watch movies, TV, and videos, do your school-work, communicate with your friends, and stay in touch with current events and the outside world?"

Daughter: "My phone and my laptop."

Me: "Just your phone and your laptop? Are there any other devices that you'd like to have?"

Daughter: "No."

Me: "What about a Smart Watch?"

Daughter: "They're stupid."

Me: "Google Glass?"

Daughter: "My friends would throw up laughing."

Me: "FitBit?"

Daughter: "Why?"

(As well she might ask. She plays three sports and eats nut butter and chia seed toast. At least she had the good manners not to suggest that *I* get a FitBit.)

Me: "iPad?"

Daughter: "It's a giant version of a phone that can't make phone calls."

Me: "iPod?"

Daughter: [rolls eyes] "Totally obsolete. The iPhone is the iPod with a phone and Internet."


The Digital Generation isn't impressed because something is high-tech. In their world *everything* is high-tech, and always has been. So much so that when my daughter was five and watching my wife trying to find the cordless phone she suggested, "Mommy, why don't you tie a string to this part of the phone and then tie the other end of the string to that part of the phone?"

**Lesson #3**
**You're better off trying to win at**
**three-card monte than you are trying**
**to predict which social media platform**
**is the best investment bet.**

Me: "Twitter is big, right?"

Daughter: "If I'm really bored."

Me: "The appeal of Twitter is supposed to be that it's immediate."

Daughter: "I haven't checked Twitter in two weeks."

[She checks Twitter.]

Daughter: "Twitter is stagnant—no one new is getting on it."

Me: "How about Facebook?"

Daughter: "Overwhelming as a whole. Cluttered. Too much oversharing. A lot of old people are on it."

Me: "Therefore, I gather Facebook is doomed."

Daughter: "No. It's the only social media where you can really get a message out, to adults and peers alike. For the memorial service at church for the victims of the shooting in Orlando, for instance. It's a big public bulletin board."

Me: "What do you use most?"

Daughter: "There's an order to it, kind of a ranking. Email is formal. I send emails to my teachers and people like that. Texting is impersonal, for checking in with parents. Also for appointments and making plans. Calling is personal. I always call my boyfriend. I use Instagram for photographs—it's less messy than Facebook, just pictures and captions. Snapchat is another way to send photographs. They disappear within ten seconds of being opened. It can be used to send nudes . . .

[shocked look on my face]

. . . but it's more permanent than people think, because you can take screenshots of the nude photos and send them all over the Internet."

Me: "Okay, that's more than I needed to know. What about advertising?"

## Lesson #4
**Internet advertising is like no advertising you've ever seen. In fact, it's like no advertising at all, possibly worse.**

Daughter: "I never look at it."

(My daughter buys things on the Internet. So does her younger sister. So does my wife. We know the UPS man so well he comes for Thanksgiving dinner.)

Daughter: "Internet ads are annoying. They're not effective. No one pays any attention to them. And I'm creeped out by the way the ads track what I've been looking at. If I'm looking at some sneakers on Amazon, all of a sudden sneaker ads start popping up. I hate them. I wouldn't buy what they're advertising."

## Lesson #5
**The Digital Generation isn't in love with the digital world.**

Factor this in whenever you hear a "brilliant idea" about using "megadata from the Internet" to "change everything."

**Daughter**: "Everything we do on the Internet is tracked, which is creepy. I'd ban that."

And the Digital Generation doesn't necessarily want to be "more connected" than it already is.

**Me**: "What do you wish was on the Internet that isn't?"

**Daughter**: "There's already too much. I really don't want to know how much time I spend on the Internet, and I really wish I didn't do it. When it's in your hand it's like automatic to go to, which I think is really bad. I hope I'll use it less in the future. I honestly have anxiety about picking up my phone."

**Me**: "You do?"

**Daughter**: "But it's mostly because of all the calls from you and Mom about where I am and what I'm doing."

# Innovation—It's All in Your Head

The most important innovations are ideas. What really changes life is more mental than material—things you hold in your mind, not things you hold in your mitts.

The most important innovation in human history was the discovery and control of fire.

Any dumb animal can discover fire . . . if it falls into a volcano or a lightning strike sets the forest ablaze. But *control* of fire—starting one, keeping one from burning down the tree you live in, putting one out—requires an animal with ideas, a humanoid.

The same is true of tools. You can find a sharp rock. Ouch—usually by stepping on it. Or you can get the notion to *make* a rock sharp. Do you put it in the fire to make it sharp? No. Do you whack it on your tree to make it sharp? No. Do you strike one kind of rock against another different kind of rock? *That's* the idea! (Even though, as I pointed out earlier, this doesn't work.)

Ideas, even dumb ideas like smacking rocks together, are the innovations that have had the greatest effect on human society.

War is an idea . . . and a reminder that innovation is not necessarily a good thing in and of itself. Every innovation is a step forward. But you might step forward into a spear point.

All primates fight, scratching and biting among themselves. But some humanoid had the innovative thought, "Instead of fighting each other, let's fight someone else."

A band of Homo sapiens was sitting around, tired of making fires and running low on mammoth meat. One of them said, "The band of *Homo neanderthalensis* in the next cave over has a fire going and lots of mammoth meat. Let's get together and kill them and take their stuff."

(I seem to be using a lot of caveman examples and analogies in my discussions of economics. It may be that there's something about economics that brings out the caveman in us all. More likely it's that I have a Fred Flintstone understanding of how the economy works. Which makes me wonder how the Hanna-Barbera animated series of the 1960s would have portrayed digital devices. William Hanna and Joseph Barbera were fond of gags involving prehistoric analogs for modern technology—a bird-beak record player, a "pigasaurus" garbage disposal under the sink. Perhaps I should be writing this book on a "laprock" with a little "microsoftasaurus" scrolling an animal hide behind a hole in the stone screen.)

Anyway . . . Agriculture and the domestication of animals were other (somewhat better) ideas.

Being a hunter-gatherer is a lot of work. One day a gatherer said, "I was wandering all over the savannah gathering grain from wild grasses. When I returned I spilled some on the ground. Now there are more wild grasses sprouting right there. Instead of wandering all over the savannah we can just sit here."

And they did. That's agriculture in a nut (or fruit or grain) shell.

Hunting is difficult too. You have to find the roaming animals. Migrating wildebeest can roam as far as a thousand miles. You have to sneak up on the wildebeest. You have to be certain of spearing the wildebeest rather than the wildebeest goring you. Then you have to drag the wildebeest meat a thousand miles back to your family.

Hunting would be much easier if the hunters could get the animals to stick around, tied up in a barn so they couldn't gore anybody.

Maybe humans tried to domesticate the wildebeest, but its first name isn't "wild" for nothing. Maybe humans tried to domesticate the cave bear. Big mistake. Maybe humans tried to domesticate the rhinoceros. Bigger mistake.

Finally, humans settled on domesticating the mouflon and the auroch. Those are the names for untamed sheep and cows when they're running around loose without a barn to be tied up in.

Sheep and cows were simple to domesticate, because they are, respectively, sheepish and easily cowed.

So now the hunters could sit around doing nothing with the gatherers. And every now and then the hunters would say, "Let's go in the barn and kill a sheep and cow."

I'm pretty sure this is how humans got the idea for civilization. They were bored with sitting around.

Very bored. How bored do you have to be before you start lugging giant blocks of stone for miles until you have so many giant blocks of stone you get the pyramids of Egypt?

And the idea of civilization didn't stop with piles of rocks. Pretty soon you had the Ancient Greeks. Their big innovation was to have ideas about *everything*.

They had the idea to put on plays—lengthy, confusing tragic dramas such as *Oedipus Rex* by Sophocles. (Spoiler alert: Oedipus dates his mother. It doesn't end well.)

They had the idea to compose a really, really long poem that doesn't rhyme, *The Iliad*. As if that weren't enough, they had the idea to compose another, *The Odyssey*.

They even had the idea to have ideas about ideas—philosophy.

Perhaps I had an ancestor in Ancient Greece. If I did, when philosophy came along, I'll bet O'Rourkopolis was saying. "Could we *please* go back to hunting and gathering?"

But we must remember the many innovative benefits of civilization . . .

And I'll think of one in a minute.

But it's a beautiful day and I'm stuck indoors with that acme of civilized innovation, Microsoft Word. I'd rather be hunting. Or, this time of year, fishing. I'll even gather, in a pinch, if there are wild blackberry bushes along the trout stream . . .

Okay, I thought of one.

The Ancient Greeks had the idea of democracy. Democracy isn't perfect, but it's an enormous improvement on how most people have been governed for most of history, from the Pharaohs to Putin.

Democracy, however, is also an example of how long it can take an innovative idea to come into widespread use, no matter how good the innovation is.

We're spoiled by living in a world of fast-forward innovation. Monday morning an idea is nothing but some blue-sky rant on an obscure tech blog. Wednesday afternoon the innovation is for sale in Walmart.

This is not the norm. It might even be a sign that we're faced with "innovation inflation" or experiencing an "innovation bubble." Ideas usually take much longer to reach fruition.

"Milk from contented aurochs" probably occurred to Australopithecus three million years ago, but nobody had a fresh glass of it until about 8500 B.C.

Ancient Greek democracy flourished in just one small city-state, Athens, with a number of tyrannical interruptions and only from 508 B.C. to 338 B.C. There's been lots of civilization since, but the idea of democracy wasn't really tried again until 1776. And after 242 years we're still working out the kinks.

We must, however, give civilization its due. Putting innovative ideas into effect would be even slower if it weren't for civilization bringing crowds of people together in small spaces.

The Latin root of the word "civilization" is *civitas*, "city." You can't have civilization without cities. Watch reruns of *Hee Haw* for proof.

When you have a city crowd you have a crowd of skills and knowledge.

Imagine James Watt inventing the first practical steam engine without a lot of skills and knowledge readily at hand.

Watt would have had to go to the Harz Mountains in Germany to dig iron ore, travel to Damascus to find the best iron smelters and to Toledo, Spain, for the finished metalwork. He would have had to go out to Mongolia to find little horses to be pit ponies and then back to Wales to put the pit ponies to work mining coal to burn to boil water.

The Industrial Revolution would never have happened. Watt would have stayed in his native Scotland blowing off steam the old-fashioned way, drinking scotch.

Civilization also makes international trade possible. There is one basic requirement for international trade: international nations. You have to have some place to trade *with*.

Just sailing over the horizon in a random way, like Columbus did, encountering scattered groups of natives, enslaving them, and giving them diseases is not an efficient mode of international trade.

It's better to know what you're doing. Cornwall has tin. France has wine. Get the two together and you have a wine-filled tin cup. Better than drinking out of your cupped hands. Much better than not drinking at all.

Yet even in a simple trade innovation like this, ideas play an important role. The old "mercantilist" idea of trade was that two-way trade was bad. Cornwall should *just* sell tin to France and not buy wine or all the money would go back to the Frenchmen.

Of course, the result of "no two-way trade" is no trade at all. All your goods are made at home and stay at home. In Cornwall they imbibe Cornish cabernet sauvignon. Ugh. In France, instead of wrapping leftovers in tinfoil, they have to stuff the leftovers through the necks of empty wine bottles, which is particularly hard with a leftover pork chop.

It took the ideas of Adam Smith in *The Wealth of Nations* to convince people that international trade was mutually beneficial to the nations involved and not some rip-off to scam their national treasuries out of money.

Adam Smith's innovative thinking opened a two-and-a-half-century era of free trade that, even more than the Industrial Revolution, enriched the world.

And this raises a third point of caution about intellectual innovation: Even the most brilliant ideas don't always last. Due to dumbbells in high places in China, the U.S., the EU, and elsewhere, our wealth-creating period of free trade may be coming to an end.

Or may be replaced with something else. Because we live in a time when wealth is, more than ever, almost completely a product of ideas.

Consider the wealthiest men of the nineteenth and early-twentieth centuries: Cornelius Vanderbilt (railroads), John Jacob Astor (fur trade), Henry Ford (Fords), John D. Rockefeller (oil refining), and Andrew Carnegie (steel, with a strong sideline in philanthropy).

This was pretty physical stuff. Take the train to Beaver Creek, Colorado, fill up the Model T with gasoline, run over a beaver, and wear the beaver hat to the opening ceremony of Carnegie Mellon University.

Now consider the wealthiest men right now: Bill Gates, Jeff Bezos, Warren Buffett, Mark Zuckerberg, and Larry Ellison.

With your Microsoft PC and Oracle database, you don't have get out of your chair to pester friends and acquaintances, purchase things you don't know what to do with, and make investments you don't understand.

It's all right not to get out of your chair. It gives you time to think. The most important innovations are ideas. Don't just do something, sit there.

# Innovations That Get No Respect

A gallon of water weighs eight pounds, five and a half ounces. Once a week I fill the poultry waterer in my chicken coop. The waterer holds five gallons. The coop is two hundred yards (one "stink distance" away) from my house. The chicken coop does not have running water.

Therefore, every Saturday morning I fill a five-gallon water can, hoist the forty-one and a half-plus pounds, and carry it . . .

Like hell I carry it. I put the five-gallon can in my tractor bucket and *drive* two hundred yards to the chicken coop.

The most important innovations are things you don't notice that are right under your nose. Or right *up* your nose—I was filling the water can from the garden hose and the water stopped running and I looked into the nozzle while my thirteen-year-old son was standing behind me un-kinking the hose.

Ready availability of water is an astounding innovation. And we take it for granted. Actually, the way we regard water is worse than taking it for granted. Recall the national hullabaloo when icky stuff started to come out of the faucets in Flint, Michigan? We regard the ready availability of water—clean, pure water—as an inalienable human right.

It's no such thing. Water doesn't come from the Declaration of Independence and the U.S. Constitution. Water comes from smart thinking and hard work.

As far as archaeologists can determine, humans didn't even begin to dig wells until around 6500 B.C. If you didn't live right next to the river, just getting the day's drinking and cooking water meant a big backache. Or a big headache, if you were balancing the water jug on your head.

The Indus Valley Civilization created the earliest public water supply system only about four thousand years ago. Water was piped directly into houses—houses, that is, of Indus Valley Civilization bigwigs. If you were an Indus Valley Civilization civilian, welcome to the town pump.

Appreciating innovations that go unnoticed in daily life is something I'm sure older readers can relate to. I'm old myself. Being old gives us a lens into the past and makes us thankful that the past *is* past.

We've used outhouses. For younger readers unaccustomed to the privy, bog, dunny, or "house of ease," imagine a port a potty that hasn't been emptied in a hundred years, where the roof leaks, and you sit on a splintery wooden board with a couple of holes cut in it and the Charmin is a corncob.

My parents were old too. My father would be 110 if he were alive. His father was born in 1877. My mother's mother was born in 1887. According to a Department of Energy study, as late as 1920 only 1 percent of American houses had indoor plumbing and electricity. (Back when being part of "The 1 percent" really meant something.)

There was, maybe, a cold tap from a cistern on the remote farms where my grandparents grew up.

Remote farms reached by way of long roads that were in turn muddy, dusty, and buried in snowdrifts. But at least they *had* roads.

We complain about our roads all the time—the traffic is horrible, the potholes are huge. But we don't stop to think (well, we do stop, but we don't think) about what an incredible innovation it is to have roads at all.

My grandmother used to tell stories about her family's innocent hayseed hired girl who was shocked by the idea of a bathtub. The hired girl said, "But a 'lady' never gets all the way undressed! She pulls up her skirt and washes her legs and pulls down her shirtfront and washes her neck."

I asked my grandmother, "Where'd the hired girl come from?"

Grandma said, "Way out in the country."

I said, "I've been to the farm. It *is* way out in the country."

Grandma said, "No, I mean way out in the country past the roads."

And this was in Illinois, not frontier Oklahoma.

The Persian Empire under Darius the Great had—his name wasn't mere flattery—great roads. Roman roads were so good that some are still in use, such as the Via Appia from Rome to Brindisi, although it wasn't so choked with Fiats during the reign of the Emperor Trajan.

So roads aren't exactly an innovation, but they are a *rein-*novation, because, during the Middle Ages, people forgot how to make a road.

How do you forget how to make a road? Beats me. It's only half as difficult as getting water to be readily available—no smart thinking required, just hard work. You put down big stones, cover them with smaller stones, cover these with little bitty stones, dig drainage ditches, and . . . Road Trip!

But people managed to forget anyway, or they got confused and began to think, "You put down big cow flops, cover them with smaller horse apples, and cover these with little bitty sheep and goat pellets."

I have just described roads all over the world until the late eighteenth century.

The "improved roads" built for the next hundred years were, in fact, no improvement on Roman roads. We'd call these roads "off-road" and put our SUVs into 4WD. Pavement of any kind was limited to city streets.

In 1900 the U.S. had 10 miles of paved country roads. We now have more than 2.6 million miles of paved roads. Next time you're stopped in traffic, think grateful thoughts about how you're not stalled in sheep, goat, horse, and cow manure.

Of course, people aren't the only things that need transporting. So does oil, gas, and electricity. Here are other parts of our infrastructure that, like roads, we don't think much about. Or don't think much about until the oil spills, the gas line blows up, or the electricity goes out. Then we get furious at the people trying to supply us with the things we want, even though we want so much of those things that leaks, explosions, and power outages are inevitable.

Yet if the people trying to supply us with oil, gas, and electricity try even harder and want to build more pipelines and high-voltage transmission towers, we get *really* furious, scream "NIMBY!" and start blogging on the Internet about how the things we want cause cancer.

And maybe they do. But do we want to be treated for cancer in a hospital without lights, heat, or air-conditioning?

The part of the taken-for-granted infrastructure that fascinates me most is the electrical grid. So many people think phone poles and power lines are unsightly. News for you folks—in the dark, everything is "unsightly."

Don't bury the power lines, lift them up on high, to remind us of our blessings.

Chief among which is the washing machine, an innovation that's surprisingly new. Electric washing machines began to be manufactured in the 1920s, but the modern "automatic washing machine," made by the Bendix Corporation, wasn't introduced until 1937. And we had to wait a year for those clothes to dry before Hamilton Manufacturing began to sell electric and gas dryers in 1938.

Early washers and dryers cost like sin. Or, I should say, they cost like washing (and drying) away the stains of sin.

When my parents got married in 1946, my grandfather gave them a washer and dryer as a very unromantic wedding present. Unromantic but not unwelcome. The pair of appliances cost about $500—$6,725 in 2018 dollars.

Hand-washing clothes is like hand-washing a car—*if* you had to lift the car and put it in a giant bucket and rub it up and down on an immense washboard until its fenders, doors, roof, grille, and trunk lid were fresh and clean. And if you had a whole used-car lot of dirty cars to wash every Monday.

Drying clothes on a clothesline is as bad or, in the winter, worse. You can't towel off . . . a towel. And a laundry basket full of wet sheets weighs as much as my poultry waterer. If I had to drag soaked and dripping bed linen from the laundry sink to the backyard clothesline, I'd be running my tractor up and down the basement stairs.

The first self-contained electric refrigerator was produced by Frigidaire in 1923. Before that, if you wanted a burger you had to cook the whole cow. And, with no place to store the leftovers, you had to eat the whole cow too.

And yet it's us now, not people back in the 1920s, who have an obesity problem. This may have something to do with the old-timers' hard labor washing and drying their clothes.

Not to mention ironing them. I tried this—once—when I was a bachelor. The ironing itself wasn't so hard, but it was a lot of work putting out the shirt fire.

Alert readers will notice that many of my examples of underappreciated innovations concern what was traditionally considered women's work in less enlightened times. And by "less enlightened times" I mean right now, when women are still doing almost all of that work.

(Power tools, by comparison, are overappreciated innovations. Try cooking, cleaning, washing, drying, and ironing with my table saw.)

Women are, as women know, underappreciated.

The greatest innovation ever, for all time, took place 1.2 billion years ago among unicellular eukaryotic organisms in the Proterozoic Eon.

Never heard of any of that stuff? Me either. I had to look it up because I'm a typical underappreciative guy. The best innovations get no respect. The Proterozoic Eon was when sexual reproduction first occurred.

Unicellular eukaryotic organisms invented women.

# Unnovations

When people say "innovation"—especially people in business and investment—they say it with a smile. They say it like they'd say "cold beer," as if it were always a good idea.

Not for breakfast it isn't. Especially not if the morning brewski is followed by smoking crack.

There are plenty of innovations—starting with crack—that need to be "*unnovated*."

## Texting

I personally would go further and get rid of all smartphones. I'm sick and tired of dealing with people whose faces are stuck in their phones.

And, yes, I'm talking to you, my three children at the dinner table.

"Huh?"

"Did you say something, Dad?"

"Sorry, I was just texting Grace. 'bles us o lord 4 these yur gifts . . .'"

Texting hits that "sour spot" between the immediacy of a phone call and emailing's speeded-up version of the post office. Put texting together with music and video delivered via personal electronic devices and *everybody's* face is stuck in the phone.

Imagine the TV show *Cheers* set in 2018. Theme song: "Where Everybody Knows Your Username." Sam and Diane, faces stuck in phones, never notice each other. Nobody yells "NORM!" or realizes that he's arrived. Waitress Carla isn't there, because drinks are ordered on menu touch screens. Woody delivers the drinks but doesn't have any funny hayseed lines. Cliff is still a know-it-all but he's posting everything he knows on his www.KnowItAll.com blog. And Frasier is busy providing virtual psychoanalysis.

## Air-Conditioning

Yes, this would be tough on people who live in hot places. But it might be worth the sacrifice. A/C is what allows Washington to operate year-round.

Ever been in D.C. in the summer? The whole city used to come to a sweltering, sticky, sweaty, somnolent halt from June through September. But now the government agencies can, with the flick of a thermostat, ruin the country fifty-two weeks a year.

As Mark Twain said, "There is no distinctly native American criminal class except Congress." (And every other branch of the federal government.)

## Government Statistics

A census is required by Article I, Section 2 of the U.S. Constitution. But the census is just supposed to count us, not ask us how many toilets we have.

The hell with the other statistics the government collects. They're just excuses for further legislative and regulatory interference in our lives. It's none of the government's business whether I'm employed. (In fact, since I haven't held a "real job" since 1981, I'm not sure myself.)

The same goes for . . .

## Political Polling

You'll recall what it got us by way of presidential candidates in 2016.

## Movie Special Effects

When special effects were limited to ketchup and blank cartridges for tommy guns we got *The Godfather*. Now, with highly sophisticated computer-generated imagery, we get *Captain America Fights the Civil War With Doctor Strange and the Guardians of the Galaxy at Spider-Man's Homecoming*.

## PowerPoint Presentations

They violate the "PowerPoint Rule": If something is so complex that it needs PowerPoint to explain it, it's too complex to be explained with PowerPoint.

## The Social Sciences

They're not science and they're not social unless you like hanging out with weird academic types. Sociology is bad chick lit. Anthropology is lousy travel writing. And Psychology is vicious gossip.

## The 24/7 Workweek

Enough already! Everybody should have a day of rest—no work, no noise, no obligations, and all communication on a strictly voluntary basis and conducted face-to-face or in pen and ink on nice paper. We need a Sabbath. This doesn't have to be a religious thing, although many sensible religions require it. The Muslims say Friday. The Jews say Saturday. The Christians say Sunday. I say "Three-Day Weekend!"

# Six Geniuses
(Plus Some Cartoon
Animators) Try to See
into the Future

How well can people predict innovation? One way to tell:
Pop open a beer, go to Amazon Video, and stream original
episodes of *The Jetsons*.

The prime-time Hanna-Barbera cartoon debuted in 1962
and was set in the "distant future" of 2062.

We're more than halfway there. It's 2018. My family should
be starting to get the innovations the Jetson family took for
granted.

They had flying cars. We have *Fast and Furious* movies
on Netflix.

They had a robot maid that was like part of the family.
We have a Roomba that the dog chased, caught, and chewed
to bits.

Their son had routine Boy Scout field trips to the moon.
My son has routine Boy Scouts field trips to . . . the field.
Where the Scouts camp out, get drenched by a thunderstorm,
and their tents collapse.

And George Jetson had a full-time job working one hour
a day, two days a week, turning his computer on and off. I

turned my computer on at 8 A.M. this morning, it's past 6 P.M., and I still have fifty-five unopened work emails.

Of course, a Hanna-Barbera cartoon is not a work of genius. Maybe we should examine some real works of genius that tried to predict the future.

A number of geniuses have attempted to forecast coming technological, economic, and social innovations.

Nobody would care to sit through an animated version of *The Wealth of Nations* by Adam Smith. But it was more accurate than *The Jetsons*.

Smith predicted the abandonment of precious metal coinage in favor of paper money to replace "a very expensive instrument of commerce with one much less costly."

Smith foretold modern central banking policy and the attitudes of the political and financial elites who shape that policy. Smith said, "The banks, they seem to have thought, were in honour bound to supply the deficiency, and to provide them with all the capital which they wanted to trade with."

Smith also gave us a warning of what would happen to "the Daedalian wings of paper money" if it became fiat currency untethered to any measure of value. In the Greek myth, Daedalus makes a pair of wax and feather wings for his son Icarus. Icarus flies too high. The sun melts the wax. And Icarus takes a plunge like the Venezuelan bolivar.

Smith is sometimes faulted for not predicting the innovations of the Industrial Revolution. He didn't predict them because he knew they were already happening. "The productive powers of labourers," Smith said, "cannot be increased, but in consequence of some addition and improvement to those machines and instruments which facilitate and abridge labour." Smith was friends with the inventor of the steam engine, James Watt.

Karl Marx was a genius too. An evil genius, perhaps, but a genius nonetheless. And he made a number of very accurate predictions about socioeconomic innovations. He was wrong about the triumph of communism, obviously. But communism was just some harebrained scheme in Marx's head. His prophesies are another matter. They're almost eerie. In *The Communist Manifesto*, published in 1848, Marx made the right call on:

*Disappearance of the middle class.* Read all about it in every news outlet.

*Confiscation of bourgeois property.* The EPA called.

*Heavy taxation.* So did the IRS.

*Liberation of women.* Done.

*Dissolution of the nuclear family.* Check.

*Working without material incentive.* "The Sharing Economy."

*Free public education.* And worth it.

*Centralization of banking and credit in the hands of the state.* Were *you* invited to the last Fed meeting?

*Combination of agriculture with manufacturing.* Chicken fingers.

*The proletariat becomes the ruling class.* Well, Trump is not exactly a proletarian, but he's not exactly "high class" either.

When we go from economic and philosophical geniuses to literary geniuses, the predictive powers seem to be fairly clear at first, then gradually become more muddled.

Jules Verne (1828–1905), the celebrated French novelist, poet, and playwright, invented the science fiction genre with works like *Twenty Thousand Leagues Under the Sea* and *Around the World in Eighty Days*. Many of the practical innovations he foresaw (submarines, air travel) were, indeed, invented.

He wrote *From the Earth to the Moon* in 1865 and *Around the Moon* in 1870. Verne was slightly off about the technical mechanisms of space travel. Shooting Apollo 11 out a cannon was not an idea that would have worked. But he was right about a Florida blastoff and a Pacific splashdown.

And, judging by what's happened since the end of the Apollo program, Verne was absolutely right about the political elite's attitude toward lunar travel innovations. He had his own elite moon-voyaging protagonists express the view that it costs too much and there's nothing up there and why bother to go again.

The American author and political progressive Edward Bellamy (1850–1898) published his utopian novel, *Looking Backward*, in 1888. By 1900 more copies of *Looking Backward* had been sold in America than of any novel except Harriet Beecher Stowe's *Uncle Tom's Cabin*.

Bellamy's protagonist arrives somehow in the year 2000 and is then filled in on the many innovations in the U.S. since Grover Cleveland was president.

Bellamy shows considerable prescience. He doesn't get things exactly right, but he comes close.

By 2000 all industries have been what Bellamy calls "nationalized." Bellamy popularized the word—he was looking for a way to avoid calling socialism "socialism." Progressives have been at it ever since, calling socialism "the Federal Reserve Bank," "FCC," "DOT," "FDI," "DOE," "USDA," etc.

Delivery of commercial goods is almost instantaneous, in case you thought Amazon was something new under the sun.

Working hours have been drastically reduced. Bellamy isn't specific about how this was done. But, these days, Facebook, Twitter, free porn sites, and computer solitaire in office cubicles have, in effect, reduced hours of actual working to a George Jetson level.

Everyone is able to retire at forty-five. Bellamy made an error here. A glance at Social Security and Medicare balance sheets indicates that nobody will be able to retire, ever.

But Bellamy was closer to reality when he describes crime as having been turned into a strictly medical problem. Isn't that what all good progressives say? Criminals aren't evil, they're sick. They need to be treated, not punished.

That's why, after my dog ate the Roomba, I didn't whack him with a rolled-up newspaper, I sent him to the dog psychiatrist for weekly sessions of "bark therapy."

Bellamy credits all the amazing innovations in *Looking Backward* to America's having become, by 2000, a socialist utopia. That, thank God, has not happened. But not for lack of trying by President Obama, et al.

The Englishman H. G. Wells (1866–1946) was Jules Verne's successor as the master of science fiction, and is best remembered for his Martian invasion book, *War of the Worlds*.

Wells was a prolific describer of the future. His 1895 novel, *The Time Machine*, takes the reader all the way to A.D. 802,701, by which time the main innovation has been Darwinian.

The working class and the elites have evolved into different species, the Morlock and the Eloi.

The Eloi are skinny, vague, naive, entitled, feckless, and childlike. They consider themselves beautiful, do nothing for a living, and eat only fruit. The Eloi are Californians.

The Morlocks are brutish ape-men troglodytes who know how to make and repair everything, do all the work, and eat Eloi alive.

We didn't have to wait 800,000 years for that prediction to come true. The Morlocks voted for Trump.

Later in life Wells became more specific about future innovations. In his 1923 novel, *Men Like Gods*, three thousand years of progress has lead to peaceful withering of the state.

Like we don't have withering of the state already, minus the peaceful.

A supposedly more advanced human race practices telepathy—as if the Internet weren't enough of a sewer dive into the minds of others.

And in 3923 A.D., there's no money. What with credit and debit cards and the Adam Smith "Daedalian wings" of the Federal Reserve, there's hardly any money now.

In 1933 Wells wrote *The Shape of Things to Come*, a suppositional history of the world from 1934 to 2016.

It is a creepy book. The biggest innovation is world government.

Think of the slaughter, misery, and oppression caused by little national governments. And a futurist hopes that expands to planetary size?

Fortunately, we've got the UN, giving us all a good laugh about the very idea of world government.

In *The Shape of Things to Come*, world government gets rid of religion, imposes an oligarchy of intellectuals, dictates the rule of "science," and does many other things that Wells seems to think are good.

If Wells had been predicting the American university campus of the future, instead of the real world of the future, he would have been a good prognosticator.

That brings us to futurism's two most famous twentieth-century works of genius—*Brave New World* by Aldous Huxley and *1984* by George Orwell—both books still being taught on those American university campuses, with great emphasis on their "relevance."

Huxley published *Brave New World* in 1931. The action takes place in the twenty-sixth century. There's a world government again (though at least Huxley has the sense to know this is not a good thing).

Rereading the book, I find it old-fashioned—more a prediction of the near present than of the distant future.

A major innovation is artificial fertilization and fetal genetic manipulation. But, instead of seeing these as progress, making for happy new parents and children free of birth defects, they scare Huxley.

Children in *Brave New World* are bred and conditioned to occupy one of five "castes"—Alpha, Beta, Gamma, Delta, and Epsilon. Or, as today's coastal elites would call them, A-list celebrities, *The New York Times* editorial board, 2020 Democratic presidential contenders, people found on Angie's List to fix the toilet, and members of the NRA.

People in the year 2540 stay youthful until the age of sixty. Hah! We've got octogenarians doing Ironman Triathlons.

All sex is strictly recreational. But S&M, B&D, LBGT and transgender sex seem not to have been discovered.

Education is conducted by a "hypnopaedic" process. Hasn't school always put kids to sleep?

High art, deep culture, and serious literature no longer exist. Ho-hum. Entertainment deals only with shallow emotions. Same old, same old. People take a drug to make them happy. Been there, done that.

In remote geographic areas, "savages" are left to their own devices. Presumably they, like the Morlocks, will vote for the twenty-sixth-century Trump in the next World Government presidential election.

George Orwell's *1984* is even more antiquated and moss-grown.

First, Orwell missed the mark by more than three decades. The real 1984 was a *great year*. Inflation had been curbed. Unemployment was falling. GDP growth was 7.3 percent (almost three times its present rate). Apple introduced its Macintosh personal computer. McDonald's sold its fifty billionth hamburger. And—"Where's the beef?"—Ronald Reagan was reelected, carrying forty-nine states.

In 1984 the U.S., thanks to a U.S.S.R. boycott, won 174 medals at the Summer Olympics. My Detroit Tigers beat the left-coast loseroid San Diego Padres 4-1 in the World Series. Hulk Hogan defeated Iron Sheik to become WWF champion.

In related news, Iran and Iraq were at war with each other instead of with everybody else in the Middle East. There were nude picture of Miss America Vanessa Williams. *TV's Bloopers & Practical Jokes* debuted on NBC. And Michael Jackson's hair caught on fire.

But since then we've caught up with George Orwell and surpassed him with our innovations, the progressives among us especially. Listen to them telling us . . .

WAR IS PEACEKEEPING.
FREEDOM IS SLAVERY REPARATIONS.
IGNORANCE IS STRENGTH IN PUBLIC EDUCATION.

*1984* has three international "superstates" in perpetual conflict and shifting alliances. We've got four, counting jihadists.

"Two Minutes Hate"? Watch *Keeping Up with the Kardashians*. Episodes last *forty*-two minutes.

And the "telescreen" that watches us while we watch it may well be where you're reading this right now.

Our students, teachers, intellectuals, public figures, and even ordinary citizens posting anonymous social media shaming don't need the "Thought Police." Policing thoughts has become a mass DIY project.

Examine any history textbook assigned in schools to see the "Memory Hole" at work on a scale undreamed of by *1984*'s protagonist Winston Smith doing his job at the Ministry of Truth turning former luminaries into "unpersons." Sally Hemings is now more revered than Thomas Jefferson.

Orwell's "Inner Party" comprised 2 percent of the population. This is double the inclusivity of the Occupy This-n-That's supposed 1 percent.

The "Ministry of Peace" is what our Defense Department has been reduced to, if even.

The "Ministry of Plenty" is, with our entitlement programs, almost our entire government.

The "Ministry of Love" is our whole political class, just ask them how they feel about you the voter when they're running for office.

And the "Ministry of Truth," like the "Thought Police," is no longer needed. Its functions have been outsourced to the aforementioned universities and *The New York Times*.

And then there's the ending of *1984*, when Winston Smith is drinking Victory Gin and staring at a "Big Brother" poster with tears of love streaming down his face—and, no doubt, wearing a red "Make Airstrip One Great Again" cap.

# A Ray of Hope in the Contest Between Man and Machine

## *What Computers Can't Do and Why There Will Always Be a Need for Stupid Humans*

In the first place, I'll start worrying about artificial intelligence when I encounter *any* intelligence.

But are computers smarter than we are?

There's something called the "Turing Test," which is supposed to determine if computers can "think." The Turing Test is a double-blind experiment to see whether a computer can fool you into thinking that you're communicating with a normal human being.

Several computer programs have passed the Turing Test.

However, Alan Turing was an English computer pioneer, logician, philosopher, and brilliant mathematician. He was one of the people at Bletchley Park who broke the German "Enigma" code during World War II. Thus it is possible that Alan Turing himself never communicated with a normal human being.

Below is a transcription of two normal human beings communicating with each other. The two humans are my middle child, a sixteen-year-old girl, and her BFF of the same age. They are communicating about a third human, a "frenemy."

**Daughter:** "She *so* did not say that"

**BFF:** "She *so* did too"

**Daughter:** "No way"

**BFF:** "Way"

**Daughter:** "I'm like OMG"

**BFF:** "LOL"

**Daughter:** "I mean, what?"

**BFF:** "On Snapchat!"

**Daughter:** "She is busted big time"

**Daughter and BFF:** [Twenty-minute fit of giggling]

Are computers smarter than humans? Most humans can't pass the Turing Test.

And this shows that there's one thing we meatbags, we skinjobs, we ugly-sacks-of-mostly-water can do that replicants, androids, synths, and all the AI on the World Wide Web will never be able to do. We can do stupid.

Humans have a lock on stupid. Computers will never understand it. You can get stupid results from computers—GIGO ("Garbage In/Garbage Out"). But it takes a human computer programmer to make it happen. Computers can think, but the smarter computers get the stupider they'll think stupidity is.

And stupid makes the world go round.

It's a big, stupid universe out there, with giant unwitting planets ignorantly spinning through moronic orbits around a thoughtless sun.

And for what purpose? To what end? The very meaning of life is stupid.

Ask yourself: What is the thing that demands stupidity, supplies stupidity, and has stupidity as its raw material and stupidity as its finished product?

The thing called love.

A handsome visage, a pretty face—it's just an iris scan to a computer. But it's everything to us. We don't care how wonderfully stupid it makes us.

Nor is our wonderful stupidity manifested only in romance. How could tottering toddlers, bumbling puppies, and kittens tangled in a ball of yarn make our hearts leap with joy if it weren't for stupidity—ours and theirs.

How could we love all creation without a stupid grin on our face?

How does 1 Corinthians, Chapter 13, Verse 13 read in the computer bible?

*So bandwidth, high throughput, and gigabytes abide, these three; but the greatest of these is gigabytes.*

Computers can't take our love away. And I don't believe computers can take our jobs away either.

Consider your job for a moment. It's probably pretty stupid. *That means a computer can't do it.*

Most jobs are stupid. My job is stupid—as you may have noticed, because here I am doing it. My job is to make stupid jokes.

I just Googled "computer-generated jokes." This is the best one I found:

**Why did the chicken cross the road?**
**To see the punch line.**

I think my job is safe.

And so is my leisure time. Computers don't possess stupidity. Therefore computers can't have fun.

Computers can't even have the most primitive immature kind of fun, such as drawing dirty graffiti on toilet stall walls. And not just because computers don't go to the toilet (no "core dump" wisecracks, please). Computers think in 0s and 1s. Here is the closest a computer can come to drawing dirty graffiti:

O

O O

I I

And the computer doesn't know this is dirty, because although computers can *store* a lot of knowledge, they don't actually *know* anything. Computers don't know that seventh-grade boys think it's funny to draw stick figures of women with large breasts unless it's been entered into their computer database. And seventh-grade boys, stupid as they are, don't input that kind of thing because Mom—who's no dummy—has keylogger software installed on their computers.

What would computer fun be like anyway? "Let's switch power supply from 120-volt house current to the 240-volt utility line *and blow our circuit breakers!*"

More probably, it's, "Let's all get together and beat Garry Kasparov at chess again." Big whoop.

There is no such thing as smart fun. Fun starts out dumb when we're little kids sticking beans up our noses and it gets dumber as we get bigger and richer.

For example, one of my favorite ways to have fun is deep-sea fishing—a sport based on my spending thousands of dollars to prove that a marlin with a brain the size of a Zippo lighter can outsmart me.

Which returns us to the Turing Test. Yes, the computer can fool you into thinking you're communicating with a normal human being. But it can't fool you into thinking you're communicating with a normal human being that you'd like to have as a buddy.

Try the "P. J. Test." Ask the computer, "Hold my beer and watch *this!*"

Now pour that beer into the computer.

Screw you, Mr. Busy Box.

# SECTION V

## Consumption

Consumption is the sole end and purpose of all
production.

— Adam Smith, *The Wealth of Nations*

Right here, boys! Right here! Get your cake, pie, dill
pickles, and ice cream! Eat all you can! Be a glut-
ton! Stuff yourselves! It's all free, boys! It's all free!
Hurry, hurry, hurry, hurry!

— The Wicked Coachman, in Walt Disney's *Pinocchio*,
welcoming stupid boys to Pleasure Island,
where they will turn into donkeys and
be sold as beasts of burden

# Introduction

## *Some Thoughts on the History of Trade*

Consumption is foremost a factor of production, of course. But the word "consumption" has an air of opulence about it. As in, "They consumed all the champagne and caviar." Champagne and caviar are imported trade goods—unless you somehow contrive to live in France and Iran at the same time. Which the Ayatollah Khomeini did. Though I don't think he drank. (Caviar is halal, however . . .)

Anyway, consumption, especially conspicuous consumption, has a strongly implied connection to imported trade goods. For that reason, before addressing consumption itself, maybe I should say something about trade. Our modern history of trade with China, for example, from where so many of our conspicuously consumed goods come.

Some may view the China trade with alarm . . .

*"OMG! The U.S. trade deficit with China is $344 billion!"*

Others with glee . . .

*"Ha-ha-ha! We got China to take $344 billion of our worthless fiat money! Suckers!"*

But no one regards China trade as unimportant.

Trade is never unimportant. Trade is how—for good or for ill—the modern world was formed. Everyone on earth is now linked to everyone else. What links us is not society or ideology. And, God knows, it's not religion. There are only two forces powerful enough to cause 7.6 billion people to hook up with each other.

One, of course, is the power of sex. But to have sex people have to be in reasonable proximity to each other (or in the same Internet chat room).

The other is the power of trade. (And that Internet chat room wouldn't exist without it.)

Trade is different from barter or exchange. Trade takes brains and guts. Barter and exchange and most other forms of buying and selling can be conducted in familiar settings.

Chimps in their trees exchange picking nits out of each other's fur.

Trade means taking your goods on the road. The root of "trade" is the Old Saxon *trada*, meaning "trail."

In order to trade you have to have some idea of why that trail is there and where it leads. Hence trade invents history and geography.

You need a notion of what kind of people are at the other end of the trail and what they want to trade for and what they have to trade with. Hence trade invents sociology and economics.

You'll require a means of communicating with those people. Hence the study of languages.

You'll want to do careful calculations about what bulk of goods can be carried on the trade route, how the goods and the necessary supplies for the trip will be transported, and the methods by which you can protect your goods and yourself. Hence math, physics, and ROTC.

Before you've even left on your trading venture, you've invented the entire college curriculum and gotten your degree.

You've also invented business. A trade expedition requires more resources than one man can provide. You'd have to be really rich to accumulate a worthwhile amount of trade goods. You'd have to be really big and strong to carry them and your gear. You'd have to be the size of an elephant. And you'd have to be more skillful than elephants are with sword, dagger, spear, and bow for fighting off robbers and brigands.

Maybe Conan the Barbarian could do it. But Conan, at least as played by Arnold Schwarzenegger, never struck me as a college man.

It's surprising that anyone ever set out to trade at all. And, at first, they probably didn't.

At first, people set out to be those robbers and brigands. They didn't trade, they just took stuff from other people and killed them all.

Then it dawned on the robbers and brigands . . . "We can't go back and take more stuff from those other people. We killed them all."

Trade has the advantage of being repeatable. Alas, as the history of the world proves, war turns out to be repeatable too. But it takes a lot longer to recover from bleeding than it does from banking your profits.

However, there's an aspect to trade that's more surprising than its existence.

Trade, while never unimportant, is often—even usually —*frivolous*.

The earliest archeological evidence of long-distance trade is found in the Middle East and dates back as far as the end of the Ice Age in 14,000 to 12,000 B.C.

The trade involved obsidian, a volcanic glass which is found in what would become modern Turkey and which wound up in Mesopotamia.

Obsidian is useful. It can be chipped to form an extremely sharp edge and provided the best cutting tool available until the Bronze Age circa 3,300 B.C.

Yet I have my suspicions about how utilitarian this obsidian trade was. Flint, readily available in Mesopotamia, can also be chipped to a sharp edge—sharp enough for practical purposes.

But maybe not sharp enough for *im*practical purposes such as circumcision.

The ancient Egyptians are known to have used obsidian knives for this "rite of passage" boys had to endure when they reached puberty.

Rites of passage—however painful—are social luxuries. X-rays of Egyptian mummies indicate that circumcision was common among the upper classes and uncommon among the poor.

Obsidian was also made into decorative objects. The poor don't decorate. Obsidian was polished into mirrors. The poor stare into a puddle when—and if—they want to know what they look like.

Plus obsidian is pretty. Flint is not.

Obsidian shows evidence of being a frivolous luxury good.

Long-distance trade was difficult, dangerous, *and* shallow, superficial, and inane.

Another well-documented ancient trade route, with beginnings in the sixteenth-century B.C., was devoted to traffic in amber.

Precious fossilized tree sap was brought from the Baltic region of Europe to second-millennium B.C. Mycenae and to Anatolia, the Levant, the Near East, and beyond. Examples of Baltic amber have been found in Han Dynasty tombs.

Amber is *useless*. The only practical application for amber is if you want to extract fossil DNA from bloodsucking mosquitoes preserved in the substance in order to clone dinosaurs and get a plot for the movie *Jurassic Park*. (Spoiler alert: This doesn't turn out well.)

It's the same with other ancient trade routes. The export of silk to Western civilizations is almost as old as the export of amber. Silk's value in the ancient Mediterranean was equal to its weight in gold. Silk was fashion-forward in the Roman Empire and has remained so ever since. You think Hermès neckties are expensive now? They cost $150 and weigh about three ounces. They'd set you back $4,000 apiece in Imperial Rome. The Silk Road wasn't called the "Burlap Bag Byway."

And the spice trade wasn't initiated because the peasants of 3,000 B.C. needed pepper in their gruel.

When Columbus bumped into the New World while trying to shortcut the spice trade, the resulting commerce was in gold, silver, and tobacco. None of which forms the basis of a healthy diet.

The truly needful and necessary products of the Americas—potatoes, corn, beans, and squash—were, at best, ballast.

The origin of trade is silly.

Jonathan Swift pointed this out in 1726 in *Gulliver's Travels*. Gulliver voyages to a country where the horses—the "Houyhnhnms"—are civilized, highly intelligent, philosophical, and wise, while the people—the "Yahoos"—are bestial, naked, semi-tamed beasts of burden.

(Off-topic aside: It is a sure sign of Silicon Valley's cultural illiteracy that a personal website provider would name itself "Yahoo.")

The Yahoos behave like typical international trade customers. Swift writes:

" . . . *in some fields of [this] country there are certain shining stones of several colors, whereof the Yahoos are violently
fond . . . they will dig for whole days to get them out, then
carry them away, and hide them by heaps in their kennels . . . [My Houyhnhnm host] said he could never discover
the reason for this unnatural appetite, or see how these stones
could be of any use to a Yahoo . . . He assured me, which I
also observed myself, that in the fields where these shining
stones abound, the fiercest and most frequent battles [among
Yahoos] are fought, occasioned by perpetual inroads of the
neighboring Yahoos.*"

Trade war!

But we owe the entire modern world and all its connec-
tions, comforts, and opportunities to "certain shining stones
[and fabrics, and ornaments, and geew-gaws] of several colors,
whereof the Yahoos are violently fond."

Trade starts out silly, but then gets down to the serious
business of consumption.

Or reasonably serious . . . I say as I stare into the shining
screen of several colors on my Apple iPhone X, made in China.

# The Price of
# Being Middle Class

*I grew up living an ordinary middle-class life.*
*What does it cost to live that life today?*

The point of consumption is pleasure.

Not an instant hot mess of pleasure . . . Well, sometimes . . . But what's much more important is the kind of pleasure that's so comfortable, homey, and wholesome that we don't
think of ourselves as "consumers" while we're consuming it.

We don't regard loving families, happy children, full stom-
achs, clad bodies, and shelter from the elements in clean, safe,
verdant places as a "product" to be "consumed."

We regard these things as natural and expected parts of
ordinary middle-class life.

But what do they really cost nowadays?

Let me go back sixty-five years to the ordinary middle-class
life I lived as a child in Toledo, Ohio, in 1952.

To calculate what 1952 incomes and prices amount to in
modern dollars, I'll use the U.S. Bureau of Labor Statistics'
basic Consumer Price Index. The CPI tells me I should mul-
tiply a 1952 dollar by 9.3 to get a 2017 dollar.

If the Tooth Fairy left a to-be-adjusted-for-inflation dime
under your pillow in 1952, you don't even have a penny now.

(Let us pause for a moment to contemplate the chilling fact that the U.S. dollar has lost 93 percent of its value in one lifetime. And pause also to wonder what other things, fundamental to an ordinary middle-class life, have lost 93 percent of *their* value. Trust in our political institutions? Patriotism? Modesty? Virtue? Faith? Hope? Charity?)

Anyway, Dad made about $10,000 a year. That's $93,000 these days. We were pretty well-off by most standards. (2017 U.S. median household income is $59,039.) And we were quite well-off by the standards of the day. (1952 U.S. median household income was $3,900.)

We had a new house with four bedrooms and a two-car garage with two cars to put into it. The house cost $21,000—which is to say, $195,300. It was in a city-suburban neighborhood, in the kind of so-called close-in suburbs that are currently getting the heck gentrified out of them, now that the 1960s–1990s crime binge has abated.

Our neighborhood was so safe that we didn't know where our door keys were—in the kitchen junk drawer, maybe.

We had three kids, a dog, and a stay-at-home mom. Stay-at-home moms were the norm. Then they became a male chauvinist oppression of women's rights. And now, I understand, they're back but are considered a lifestyle luxury.

The public schools were excellent. The grade school was a block away. Everybody walked. Nobody was dropped off by a nanny. We didn't know from nannies. Maybe a nanny was Billy Goat Gruff's little sister?

In first grade Miss Westfall had us reciting the alphabet forward *and* backward. In fourth grade Miss Sonnenberg made us memorize the multiplication tables through 13 times 13. Miss Geiger, the principal, told us, "All I require is that when I say 'Jump', you ask 'How high?' on the way up."

The high school was three blocks away. It taught calculus but also home ec, Latin but also shop. It had a state championship football team.

The high school sent its share of students to places like the University of Michigan, and every year a few went to the Ivy League. Although, if you told your neighbors in Toledo, "My son is going to Princeton," they would say, "Why? It's so far from home."

Toledo was in the "Rust Belt." But in those days the Rust Belt was more like the "Cummerbund of Steel"—the center of American industrial production.

Toledo was the corporate headquarters for Willys Jeep, Champion Spark Plug, Autolite Batteries, DeVilbiss Paint Spray Guns, and Toledo Scale. It was the largest soft-coal port in the nation. It was called "The Glass Capital of America" because the Libbey-Owens-Ford, Owens-Illinois, and Owens Corning glass companies were all based there. Business and employment opportunities abounded.

Now let me try to figure out how and where an ordinary 1952 middle-class Toledo, Ohio, life could be lived in 2017.

It has to be in a place that's hip and has a strong economy. Toledo was never hip. But in 1952 it was hip to be square. And Toledo was very square. So the modern equivalent would have to be someplace like Portland, Oregon.

Portland's median household income is above average. Its unemployment rate is below average. Portland is, as Toledo was, on the cutting edge of what's contemporary in technology. Portland is sometimes called "Silicon Forest" for its abundance of tech firms. (And for all the nearby trees that hipsters love, like the squares of yore loved wide-open spaces—which Toledo had in plenty, with cornfields growing right up to the city limits.)

Portland is twice as populous as Toledo was in 1952, but the whole USA is twice as populous now. And, in the "Things We Don't Talk About Department," Portland is very white (72 percent), about as much so as Toledo was in my boyhood—if you count the Irish as white.

I searched the Internet real estate listings for a home in a Portland city-suburban neighborhood. Healy Heights seems to have the lowest crime rate and the best public schools. Other people have noticed this too. Only six houses were for sale. The best deal I could find for a four-bedroom with a two-car garage was $650,000.

It's a little more posh than the house I grew up in, but having been built in the 1970s Leftcoast Modern style . . .

*Throw away the level and plumb-bob! Put the windows any-where! Let a crazy person draw the roofline! Slap up the wood siding every-which-way!*

. . . it is a lot more ugly.

Mortgage rates were close to the same in 1952 as they are now. Dad's monthly mortgage payment was probably about $100—$930 in chained dollars. The Healy Heights mortgage payment is estimated at $2,536.

Now to shop for two cars. Dad's 1952 Buick Super Riviera Sedan cost $2,563 ($23,836), and Mom's '52 Chevy station wagon cost $2,297 ($21,362). But you can't fit three kids and the giant backpacks all kids carry everywhere these days into a modern sedan, especially not if you're taking them on the requisite snowboarding trip to Mt. Hood. (The 1952 Toledo equivalent: ice fishing for carp on Lake Erie.)

The sedan will have to be an SUV. I guess the BMW is the Buick of today; an X5 goes for $56,600. And it's Portland, so

Mom gets a Prius, $23,475. (Note that that's what it used to cost to buy a Buick, a big, swoop-fendered, port-holed, chrome-bedazzled, beautiful Buick. And now you get . . . a Prius.)

It's fairly easy to calculate the cost of comparable housing and transportation. Comparing the cost of food and clothing is more difficult, so I've left them out. Styles shift. Men's suits cost about the same, adjusted for inflation. But who wears a suit anymore? And I Googled "men's luxury T-shits" and found a Salvatore Ferragamo crew neck selling for $220 at Saks Fifth Avenue. Adjust for inflation all you want, but nobody in 1952 was going to pay like that for underwear.

Tastes in food have changed as well, and getting over-scheduled moderns to all sit down at the same time for a home-cooked dinner is almost impossible. Equally impossible is getting moderns to stay out of trendy restaurants.

Nonetheless, food has gotten relatively cheaper. According to the Bureau of Labor Statistics, in the 1950s an average household spent twice as much of its budget on food as it does now (32 percent versus 15 percent).

Food, however, is about the only thing that's gotten cheaper in ordinary middle-class life.

Partly this is because we expect more from that life. We expect vacations.

An all-included trip to Beaches Ocho Rios Resort in Jamaica for a family of five, plus airfare from Portland to Kingston and a generous tip to the cabana boy because of what the kids did in the pool, is $9,581.75.

Not that we didn't take vacations in 1952. We went to my uncle's cottage on the lake. That cost (steaks + case of beer + fill up car + carton of night crawlers for bait) $23.25.

Then there is the true killer of the middle class—being schooled to death.

As I mentioned, Portland's Healy Heights neighborhood has the best public schools in the city. Of course it does. We wouldn't move our families into anyplace that didn't have the best public schools. But it's not as if we're actually going to *send our children there*. Heaven forbid!

Public schools are full of bullies. Public schools don't teach Mandarin. Classrooms are crowded. The other children get head lice. The gym doesn't have squash courts. PE does not include sailing instruction.

The best public schools are there *just in case*. Just in case little Liam or little Ava have "issues" and are required to leave the best private school.

The best private school in Portland is the Catlin Gabel School. K-12 tuition is $29,640 per child.

Now, let's do the math.

| Annual Expenses, in 2017 Dollars, for a Family of 5 Leading an Ordinary Middle-Class Life in 1952 | | Annual Expenses for a Family of 5 Leading an Ordinary Middle-Class Life in 2017 | |
|---|---|---|---|
| Mortgage Payments | $11,160.00 | Mortgage Payments | $30,432.00 |
| New Car Purchases (amortized over 5 years) | 9,039.60 | New Car Purchases (amortized over 5 years) | 16,015.00 |
| Family Vacation | 216.23 | Family Vacation | 9,581.75 |
| Education | 0.00 | Education | 88,920.00 |
| **TOTAL** | **$20,415.83** | **TOTAL** | **$144,948.75** |

And one last thing . . . Because the divorce rate has doubled since 1952, there is a very good chance that an ordinary middle-class life will include a divorce. Get divorced, start a new family, and the cost of being middle-class is multiplied by two: $289,897.50

What the math tells us is . . . *In order to live an ordinary middle-class life, you have to be rich.*

# Armchair Predictions About Consumer Trends

I am strictly an armchair observer of consumer trends. My predictions don't come from deep knowledge or brilliant analysis—they come from the seat of my pants. Literally.

Let me explain.

I make my predictions based on what I see and hear sitting in a chair in my living room. My family happens to contain an ideal consumer focus group—two young millennial daughters.

This demographic is responsible for a large portion of America's consumer spending. From what I can tell by my credit card bills, my daughters do about 120 percent of that spending.

It's important to know what my focus group is (and isn't) buying.

That's where my armchair comes in. I like to sit there in the evening reading the newspaper and having a drink. Or, given what the news has been like lately, a couple of drinks.

However, I live in a house with a stupid floor plan. At one end is a large family room where my daughters do their homework, fiddle with their electronic devices, and watch TV. At the other end is the kitchen, where my daughters make snacks and a mess. And the only way to get from the family room to the kitchen and back is by way of the living room, through which they constantly traipse.

I don't get much peace and quiet, but I do get to see both daughters frequently and overhear things about what they want and don't want, like and don't like, and are or aren't planning to do.

Lately I've been paying attention to this information, as it applies to consumer spending.

My nineteen-year-old daughter is a living issue of *Vogue* magazine except more interested in clothes. If you're wondering where all the weird getups from New York Fashion Week go after the runway shows, they're in her room. How she gets dressed in there I don't know. The room is so full of clothing that there's no space for the girl who wears it.

And yet (all kidding about my credit card bills aside), my daughter is remarkably frugal. She pays for most of her clothes herself with wages from a none-too-lucrative after-school job.

I could not figure out where her clothes were coming from. I was beginning to worry. So, as she passed from kitchen to family room wearing something that Lady Gaga had rejected as too out-there, I asked. And my daughter set me straight about her generation's shopping habits.

She and her friends—and, from what I can tell, millions of other girls their age—are on the Internet constantly buying and selling and trading their clothes to each other. My daughter's room isn't just filled with clothes. It's also filled with UPS boxes, some being opened, some being packed.

They look at fashion magazines, blogs, and YouTube videos to get high-style ideas, then network with fellow young "fashionistas" to find low-price knockoffs. Or they alter existing garments to get what's chic. Some make clothes themselves. Others paw through the racks at Goodwill stores for vintage finds. They wear their outfits a few times, then pass them along at bargain rates.

My daughter visits department stores, boutiques, and malls, but mostly to check fabrics, quality, and sizes. My daughter goes to Bloomingdale's the way I go to a Ferrari dealership. Which Ferrari would be just right for me? In my dreams!

My prediction is that the retail clothing business aimed at young women (a big part of the retail clothing business) had better wake up and smell the packing tape on the UPS boxes.

For decades this retailing, both in-store and online, has been based on the idea that girls are voracious and vacuous shoppers who regard clothing as essentially disposable and compulsively buy new things. The girls have found a way to fight back.

My sixteen-year-old younger daughter is less interested in clothes, possibly because she goes to a school with a boring dress code. But she is an avid consumer of personal electronic communication in its every form.

I'd often see her, as she walked by my armchair with an armload of devices, texting, emailing, tweeting, Snapchatting, Skyping, checking Facebook, and talking on the phone at the same time.

Then one evening she came in, sat down on my footstool, and poured her heart out. With big sad eyes, she told me it was over, done, they were breaking up—she and personal electronic communication.

She said, "I just can't stand it anymore! It's like having everybody you've ever met on permanent sleepover at your house forever! All the whispering, giggling, gossiping, and pillow fights . . . I mean *virtual* pillow fights . . . have just got to STOP!"

I questioned her gently, expecting to hear mean-girl stories or reports of unwelcome Instagram photos of boys in their underpants.

But her concerns had a greater maturity than that. "Dad," she said, "what I really can't stand is all the political stuff everybody is sending all the time. It's so angry. It's so, like, *loud*."

Here is a girl who goes to a liberal private school, but who grew up in conservative rural New Hampshire and was raised by parents with firm libertarian/conservative principles. She has friends and family with political views of every conceivable stripe. Until now this had never bothered her. She just thought she lived in a diverse world where reasonable people had reasonable disagreements . . . Until she encountered "Communication Overload."

She said, "Dad, it's worse than a permanent sleepover. I mean there's lots of that too, and it drives me nuts. But now it's like the school debate team. Except *everybody* from *everywhere* is on this debate team. And everybody's making their debate argument all at once at the top of their lungs and nobody's in the audience, there is no audience, *nobody's listening!*"

I didn't know what to say. Finally I told her, "Well, I suggest you stop listening too."

"I'm going to," she said. "I'm turning *everything* off."

Which, of course, she didn't do. She still chats on her iPhone and sends texts to her friends with a blur of young thumbs. But I notice she is, indeed, spending less time with her devices.

My guess is that her Communication Overload would have come anyway, even without the current political fracas.

Constant communication deprives us of an important part of communication—the part where we pause between communications and have time to accumulate experiences, knowledge, and thoughts that are worth communicating.

My prediction is that someday we will look back on the personal electronic communication fad with as much bafflement as we look back on the Hula-Hoop. We'll consider being in constant communication with each other to be as silly and (unless you permanently injured your spine during the Hula-Hoop craze) more dangerous.

My armchair advice is that, next time you hear about an IPO for an app that will make it easier for the whole world to get in touch with my younger daughter, keep your investment money in the pocket of the perfectly tailored cashmere cardigan sweater that my older daughter can get you for $15.

# Consumer Trends Among the "Grumpies"

I have a perfect demographic focus group of millennial female consumers right in my living room.

But now I've realized I've also got a perfect demographic focus group of another segment of consumers: the male sixty-five-plus baby boomer. That focus group is me.

I'm a *real* armchair expert on this subject, because I'm the one sitting in the armchair.

Marketing experts don't seem to think of guys like me as being major consumers. To judge by advertising that's pitched to people our age and gender, you'd think the only things we shop for are Medicare supplemental insurance, reading glasses, and Viagra.

The marketing experts are fools. In fact, male sixty-five-plus baby boomers are more important to U.S. consumer economics than most other sections of the population, including the Yuppies.

Call us the "Grumpies"—*Graying Rich Upset Male Persons*.

And note the "rich" part. What makes us important is that we've got the money. Men over the age of sixty-five are among the Americans with the highest average net worth. (That is, if we're still alive. The Americans with the highest average net worth are the *widows* of men over sixty-five.)

So pay attention, marketing experts. (And investors too.) Keep an eye on Grumpie consumer trends.

Of course, given that the main characteristic of Grumpies is grumpiness, these are not "consumer trends" in the sense of "products we want to buy." These are gripes—consumer trends in the sense of "products we'd like to stuff up the noses of the people who manufactured them.

But the companies that marketing experts work for don't make profits just by knowing what products consumers love. They also need to know what products consumers loathe.

And here are some . . .

We don't like the Internet. Of course it's handy, and, like everybody else, we use it all the time. But . . . When we're trying to Google something important, such as "best salmon river in Atlantic Canada," and an ad pops up . . . The way we feel about the company that posted that ad is the way Gloria Steinem feels about Bill O'Reilly.

We Grumpies hate social media. (Even if your little Suzy and that dork she married do put cute pictures of the grand-kids on Facebook.)

In fact, we detest the whole everybody-connected-to-everybody-24/7 thing. We'd like to be *disconnected*, up on the Miramichi in New Brunswick casting flies and claiming that our cell phones and laptops fell out of our waders.

We'd also like someone to develop an app that gets rid of all apps, a no-app app; call it a "napp."

Maybe that would keep people from fiddling with their phones all day. Imagine Stanley missing Livingston in darkest Africa because they both had their noses buried in their iPhones. "No cell service, I presume."

No one is willing to dispose of their phones these days. Meanwhile everything else that's for sale seems to be completely disposable, and this makes us Grumpies mad.

When I moved to rural New England in the 1970s, I bought a bunch of power tools. Forty years later, they still work. Albeit my old Skillsaw is down to about 60 rpm. And, with my original electric drill, I keep forgetting to take the chuck wrench out of the chuck, causing the chuck wrench to fly across my shop and bust a window.

So I bought a good cordless drill a few years back. But its battery packs have quit taking a charge. I went to the hardware store to buy new batteries and found out they'd have to be special-ordered. *If* they still made those batteries anymore, which the hardware store clerk wasn't sure about.

Then I found out I could buy a new drill, the same brand, with a pair of different "improved" battery packs, for less than what the special-order batteries for my old (perfectly satisfactory) drill would cost.

This is just wrong. Shortly afterward, my Shop-Vac died— the 50-cent plastic on/off switch broke. And, you guessed it—the price to get it fixed was more than the price of a new Shop-Vac.

Build things to last, damn it! We Grumpies may not be children of the Depression, but we're children of children of the Depression, and we grew up hearing: "Use it up, wear it out, make it do, or do without."

I couldn't fix the Shop-Vac myself because . . . (A) They don't make that (perfectly satisfactory) model of Shop-Vac anymore . . . (B) They don't make parts for that model of that Shop-Vac anymore . . . And, (C) When I tried to substitute another switch I laid a screwdriver across the positive and negative poles to test the connection and set off all the smoke alarms in my shop.

Okay, maybe point (C) was my bad . . . But you can't fix *anything* anymore.

You can't even comprehend it.

The washer, dryer, and dishwasher at our house have no knobs or dials. Instead they have circuit boards that look like miniature maps of downtown Mumbai faced with flat panels of electronic touch controls—you touch them and they take control. What will happen next is anyone's guess. The washer dries, the dryer sets itself on "rinse," and the dishwasher goes into spin cycle.

Same with cars. Unfixable. I grew up in the automobile business. I was a passable shade tree mechanic in my youth. But now I'm flummoxed. I don't even try anymore. The last time something started to go *thunk-thunk-thunk* I didn't bother to look in the engine compartment, I immediately took the car to a real mechanic.

My mechanic is a Grumpie too. He's been working on cars since the Edsel was the Tesla of its day. I can speak frankly with him.

I opened the hood and said, "To tell the truth, I don't know what two-thirds of the stuff in here is."

My mechanic said, "To tell the truth, I don't either."

# Consumer Trends Among the "Grumpies," Part 2

*Could I Please Get a Plain, Regular Car?*

There are lots of us Grumpies. And we hate all of today's overcomplicated, electronics-infested, instantly obsolete, un-fixable, fiddle-faddle-f\*\*\*-it consumer products.

I mentioned cars. Specifically I meant to say that it takes an MIT triple doctorate in computer science, electrical engineering, and quantum physics to open the hood of a modern car and know what you're looking at.

Grumpies have given up looking under the hood. Except maybe to add windshield wiper fluid, and sometimes it takes a trained technician in a dealership service department to do that. We know we're going to be flummoxed by the engine compartment.

It used to be there was just an engine block in there with a carburetor on top, a radiator in front, plus an alternator and exhaust manifolds. Now, emissions regulations, fuel efficiency standards, and a proliferation of federally mandated automatic sensors mean we're faced with a pollution control plumber's nightmare and a mare's nest of wiring harnesses, all sprinkled with the fairy dust of computer chips.

More and worse is on its way, with new forms of power train technology such as cars that run on renewable wind and solar energy. The solar energy will come from your car getting broiling hot inside while it's locked and sitting in the sun in the mall parking lot. The wind energy will come from the breeze through the window that the opioid addict smashed to snatch your phone.

But just because the innards of an automobile have become a skunkworks—repellent to the minds of ordinary guys—doesn't mean that the rest of the automobile has to annoy the hell out of us too.

I want a plain, regular car—no parking assist, no lane-drift alert, no reality TV show about what's happening behind me on the touch screen, and no damn touch screen either, and absolutely no voice-activated anything. I've got a black Lab called Georgie and I don't want Amazon's Alexa playing Boy George music every time I tell my retriever to quit knawing on the upholstery.

Also, no GPS. I know where I am. I'm right here. And I know where I'm going. I'm going home. It's cocktail hour.

I'm not alone in my desire for a gizmo-free, gadget-purged vehicle. On May 11, 2017, *The Wall Street Journal*—a publication with plenty of Grumpie readers—ran a front-page feature titled, "Your New Car's Best Tech Feature May Be the 'System Off' Button," and subtitled, "Buggy software, touchy touch screens baffle drivers."

I bet I'm also not alone in the particular kind of plain, regular car I want. We Grumpies tend to hunt and fish and otherwise putter around in the outdoors. We own property, tow boats, keep animals, plant shrubs, have families, etc. We want a big, honking SUV.

I live in remote rural New England with a wife, three children, three dogs, and all the sporting goods and leisure equipment that comes with them, plus my beer cooler.

In fact, I've already got a big, honking SUV. It's a Chevy Suburban, one of five or six I've owned over the past twenty years. Suburbans are good cars—commodious, sturdy, and reasonably priced if you buy them, like I do, off lease after 30,000 miles of gentle (and, as it were, *suburban*) use as glorified minivans for soccer moms.

But the Suburbans, like all other full-size sport-utilities, are too gussied up. I have to sell mine at around 125,000 miles (which is about when a 1960s-era Suburban was getting broken in) because all their tech geew-gaws start getting squirrels in the attic.

I'd like to make a deal with manufacturers. I'll buy a brand-new Chevy Suburban (or Ford Expedition or Toyota Sequoia or Lincoln Navigator or Jeep Grand Wagoneer or whatever) and pay a large premium over suggested retail price *if* the car has the following features. (And lacks the features I've complained about already.)

*Clearance.* My local roads are so bad that the only way to tell "off-road" from "on-road" is that I encounter fewer trees in the middle of the roads than I encounter in the middle of the forests unless there's been an ice storm and all the trees have fallen into the roads. Speaking of which, winter around here lasts thirteen months a year.

I don't just drive *on* stuff. I drive *over* stuff. And *through* stuff. Getting to the best bird covers and most productive trout pools can be hell, and you don't get there on the proverbial wide road paved with good intentions.

Over the years full-size SUVs have lost clearance as they've acquired more sophisticated, less trucklike suspensions to provide a smooth ride. Midst the potholes, frost heaves, and fallen trees of rural New England, there *is* no soft ride. You're the dash of vermouth in a martini shaker no matter where you're going.

*No carpeting.* On *any* surface. Due to New England's horrible weather, I use my SUV as an "indoor pickup truck." I load bales of hay in the back. The sidewalls of the cargo compartment are lined with something from the looms of the Bigelow mill. Why? No car vacuum ever made will extract the embedded bits of hay from the carpet pile. Every time I look in the back I'm reminded of 1968 when my friend Groovy was trying to fill the bong, tripped over the lava lamp, and spilled the baggie of stems and seeds into mom's rec room shag rug.

*Interior volume.* Because my SUV is an indoor pickup truck, I don't need the third row of seats. (I figure if you're hauling around more than three kids, three dogs, and a spouse, you should get a school bus or birth control.) What I do need is space to lay a four-by-eight sheet of plywood flat. My Suburban is two and a half feet too short, and it's the longest SUV on the market. Come on, GM, these cars are already the length of cruise ships; what's an extra thirty inches? Are you afraid you won't be allowed to dock in Fort Lauderdale?

*Ready to get hosed.* I want to clean the inside of my car with a power washer. I mentioned I have kids and dogs. This means cola spills, gum wads, ice cream drips, and vomited rodents. I want metal floors and door trim panels, rubber mats, waterproofed dials and gauges, and all my upholstery including the headliner covered in heavy-duty vinyl that the retriever can't chew.

P.S. I have an ancient Jeep with a simple but brilliant accessory long forgotten by modern car-makers. In the Jeep's foot wells there are inch-wide rubber plugs. Pull the plugs and you get drain holes.

P.P.S. Some machine-washable elastic slipcovers would be welcome too. Make them the color of dog hair and sticky kid snacks.

*Stick shift.* So the kids will be less tempted to borrow my car. Kids today don't know how to drive stick shift. At least my kids don't. They watch me shift gears and say, "Isn't there an app for that?" (And, with modern electronically controlled automatic transmissions, alas, there is.)

*Bench seats.* Ditch the center console and give me some room for petting and necking. My retriever likes to cuddle. As it is, she's got her rear paws stuck in the cup holders and her front paws on the dashboard, and she gets a snootful of rearview mirror every time we come to a sudden stop.

While you're at it with removing the center console . . . *Put the shifter back on the steering column.* There's nothing wrong with "three on the tree." If I've got a transfer case that gives me high and low 4WD I don't need every gear ratio known to man.

*And don't even think about making my car a "driverless car."* I'll do the driving, thank you very much. Also, those three kids of mine are teenagers. Have you ever watched teens behind the wheel? They're messing with their phone texts, fussing with their iPads, talking to one friend while Skyping with another, and trying to conceal cans of cold beverages that they're not legally old enough to buy. For me, that's plenty enough of a "driverless car."

# Summing Up American Consumer Trends . . .

On my desk I have a pile of statistics about "consumer trends." A bunch of numbers: such and such percentage increase or un-crease in this, that, or the other median doohicky of whatchama-callems and thingamabobs from way back when to lately, according to the National Bureau of Whoosis and Whatzat.

I'm throwing the statics in the wastepaper basket.

A better way to understand American consumer trends is simply to observe America—just look around and open your eyes . . . and your ears.

We're purchasing a lot more unholy racket. The seasons used to change to the tune of gentle sounds. Fall arrived with the rustle of leaves and the shuffle of leaf rakes. Winter meant silent snow and soft scrapes of front walks being shoveled. Spring came with the modest clatter of dad rummaging in the garden shed for trowels and clippers. And when was the last time you heard the soothing *snick-snick* of a push lawnmower?

Now it's the tornado howl of leaf and snow blowers, the roar of rider mowers with engines powerful enough to compete at the drag strip, and the crash, bang, and shouts of yard care crews in the tiny yard of your giant McMansion. A yard you never set foot in because if you want to see what's outdoors you've got a security camera you can watch on your phone.

Another consumer trend that is *widely* apparent . . . I mean half of the 380-pound person in the middle seat on my airline flight is spilling into my personal space . . . is food.

How did Americans get so huge? Rhetorical question. Drive down any commercial strip. Where there once was a diner, a White Castle, and a truck stop there is now . . .

Cowabunga Burger . . . Fatty Fries . . . Chunk-Up Chicken . . . Cheesy Chef . . . Gobble King . . . Beef Blimp . . . Taco Dump . . .Double-Butt Pizza . . .

Americans not only look gross, but they dress the part. We've become a nation of immense nine-year-olds dressed for all occasions in T-shirts, shorts, and Tevas. Or, sometimes, just to change things up, pajama pants, sports bras, and wife-beater shirts.

The clothes are revealing, but in no erotic sense. What's revealed are big, hairy legs and vast ass tattoos.

The number of clothing stores in malls, the amount of clothing shopping on the Web, and the pile of clothing catalogues arriving in the mail indicate that Americans are acquiring all sorts of clothes. Why aren't they wearing them?

Americans are also acquiring more personal communication devices than there are persons. Walk into any public place and everyone is staring into a screen. There's no one to talk to. There's no longer any chance of striking up a friendly acquaintance in a waiting room, train, plane, or bar. Even when conversation does occur in a bar, the lively debate about who played shortstop for the 1986 Chicago Cubs is cut short by some fool Googling it. (Shawon Dunston.)

With whom is everyone communicating? If it's people he or she knows already, haven't they long ago run out of things to say? Or are they all on dating sites . . . and never noticing the attractive person sitting next to them?

Maybe they're checking the news. Presumably the people who run the news business—online, print, TV, and radio— present the news the way consumers want it. Therefore a significant American consumer trend is a bull (not to say bullshit) market in shallow, sensationalist, and often errone-ous news stories.

All these stories are terrifying—by intent. "If it bleeds it leads" is a news business maxim. You'll never see a headline about how good things are. Especially not involving President Trump. His ability to grab the public's attention irks the news business, which thinks it should have a monopoly on grabbing the public. (Per Matt Lauer.)

Thus, if Donald Trump cured cancer, the headlines would read, "Heart Disease Kill More People."

We don't have to look far to see that something else being consumed in enormous quantities is drugs. Marijuana has been legalized all over the place, as is evident in the vacant stares of millennials as they try to remember what the bike rack is for.

Emergency rooms are filled with unemployed former blue-collar workers using opioids to get too happy, then too desperate, then too dead, then resurrected with Narcan, then too happy again.

To be a white-collar worker is, almost definitionally now, to be on some kind of antidepressant. You can tell by how nobody beats on the copier anymore when there's a paper jam. People just give the copy machine a sad smile of fellow feeling.

Traffic is terrible, airports are packed to bursting, and so is mass transit. "Transportation" is obviously a fast-growing segment of consumption. But not transportation to the office. More and more employees are working from home.

Yet, walk down the street in your neighborhood knocking on doors. Nobody's *at* home. Brick-and-mortar stores claim crowds are thin. Schools say truancy is up. Where are all the people going? To judge by the stalled cars, canceled flights, and broken-down subway cars—nowhere soon.

In considering the current American decibel level, body mass index, sartorial appearance, Internet connectivity, high anxiety, chemical ingestion, and traffic jams, we see a clear pattern of consumer trends.

What Americans are buying is noise, fat, naked shame, loneliness, fear, stupor, and futile attempts to escape from consumer society.

# All the Money
# in the World

What would I do if I had a $100 billion?

These things can happen to a person . . . Well, so far, to only one person—Jeff Bezos. But you know . . .

"*Everything you imagine, you can do*," I'm told. (Or, rather, my kids are told, ad infinitum, in their progressive, positive-learning-experience schools with 90 percent of classroom time spent teaching self-esteem.)

Years ago I did do *something*. I wrote an article with a really great title, if I say so myself: "How to Drive Fast on Drugs While Getting Your Wing-Wang Squeezed and Not Spill Your Drink." (It was written for a humor magazine.) (I was kidding.) (Sort of.) (I was twenty-nine.)

Maybe "*How to*" . . . is made into a blockbuster movie, a bestselling video game, a hit song that stays at #1 on the Billboard Hot 100 chart for fifty-two weeks, a wildly successful brand of legalized pot, the go-to craft beer for millenials, a killer app, an Internet search engine, and the largest hedge fund on earth: "Drive Fast on Drugs While Getting Your Wing-Wang Squeezed and Not Spill Your Drink, LLC."

And I make $100 billion. After taxes.

What would I do?

Take a nap.

Why not? Making a lot of money is sort of like discovering a miracle diet. It's an Instant Worry-Loss Program. Very relaxing. And when I'm very relaxed I like to take a nap.

I'll never worry about going broke again. (Which gives me more time to worry about dying and about my kids getting facial piercings, full sleeves of tats, and marrying Louis C.K. But never mind.)

After my nap I'll buy some things I've always wanted.

But . . . mmm . . . I'm seventy. I've kind of already done that.

I don't want a new house. We've been in our place for twenty-five years. It's nothing that would be featured in *Architectural Digest*, unless they do a special issue on "Run-of-the-Mill Old Federal-Style Houses with Ugly Additions from the 1980s." But I've *almost* figured out how the plumbing and septic systems work. I don't want to go through that again. Also, the dogs like it here.

I certainly don't want a new wife. I love mine. (What's with "trophy wives"? What do you *do* with a trophy wife? Set her on the mantel next to my JV Bowling Team cup for "Most Improved"?) Also, I know for sure my present wife didn't marry me for money, because I for sure didn't have any when we got married.

(I should, however, check to see whether this is a "community property" state. My wife might not feel the same way about getting a new me.)

I have golf clubs, skis, shotguns, and power tools—all of them better in quality than my golfing, skiing, bird-hunting, and . . . the shelves I built in the garage just came crashing down.

I have an ample supply of good scotch due to having turned seventy. Nobody knows what to give a seventy-year-old man for his birthday except a bottle of good scotch. (Right choice.)

I have a couple of old classic cars to tinker with. Well, they're not classics, but they are old. I wouldn't know how to tinker with an $8 million 1958 Ferrari Testarossa and its twelve cylinders, four overhead cams, and six two-barrel Weber carburetors. I wouldn't even dare to check the tire pressure.

I'll get a pickup for the farm—$40,000.

(Jeez! When I first moved to the country you could get a new pickup for five grand.)

I'll ask my wife if she'd like an upgrade on her 2014 Volvo XC90. But I know what she'll say. "A Porsche Cayenne is too flashy for New England." (Bless her heart.) I'll get her a 2018 Volvo XC90—$50,000.

I'll replace the 2004 Volvo XC70 station wagon that we've got for our teenagers to bang up by backing into phone poles, colliding with other cars in mall parking lots, and driving into ditches . . .

On second thought, no I won't.

I'll buy a John Deere backhoe because . . . Because I've always wanted one. (You can tell the age of the boy by the size of the toy.) It'll make weeding the herbaceous borders a snap next spring—$100,000.

Okay, so far I've spent $190,000.

I suppose my wife will want to go shopping. But, again, I know what she'll say: "Prada's too flashy for New England. I'll stick to Target."

(I won't add in any shopping for my three teens. How much do ripped jeans cost? You can get them for free if you raid the Planet Aid donation box.)

Now I've spent $190,159.95. That leaves me $99,999,809,840.05 to go. I'd better get busy.

A private plane? A luxury yacht? I have an old friend who's a pilot and a sailor (and who's been divorced three times). He says, "If it flies, floats, or . . . [Let's not go there with what his third f-verb is] *rent it!*".

A pied-a-terre in the city. So Mrs. O'Rourke and I can go to town and have some fun! (A small place, so that we *can't* bring the kids.)

The Pierre Hotel, at Fifth Avenue and 61st Street in New York, is selling a four-room condominium apartment on a high floor overlooking Central Park—$5,000,000.

A beach shack to escape New England's lousy winters, big enough for family, friends, dogs, friends' dogs, etc.

I like Sanibel Island on the Gulf Coast—unspoiled "Old Florida." And here's just the thing on Zillow: eleven thousand square feet with seven bathrooms and seven hundred feet of private beachfront—$22,000,000.

Oh yeah, college for my children. It's not the tuition; that's a drop in the bucket. It's getting my kids *into* college. My kids are—like everybody's kids—brilliant, of course. But, like their old man, they . . . um . . . To quote from a recent parent-teacher conference, ". . . have tremendous potential but with room for considerable improvement in effort, concentration, and study habits . . ."

In other words, they ain't getting into Harvard.

*Unless . . . maybe . . .* I match or exceed the largest-ever gift to Harvard, $400 million, made by hedge fund billionaire (and "Big Short" beneficiary) John A. Paulson in 2015.

But who the hell wants kids who go to Harvard? As if they're not smart-asses enough already. I have no desire for children like Al Franken (Class of '73).

Instead, I send them to a good state school such as Miami of Ohio, where I went. "Or," my wife will say, "a *better* state school, such as Indiana University, where *I* went."

(Hah! Ben Roethlisberger played for the Miami RedHawks. Who's in the NFL's "Hoosiers Who's Who"? Babe Laufenberg. Starting QB for the 1988 San Diego Chargers. He threw four TDs and five interceptions in six games before being sacked by the Saints and getting his ribs crushed.)

But I digress . . . The new gym at Miami cost $14 million. Title IX probably means they need another one: "The O'Rourke Family C Students Sports Pavilion." I can get my kids into Miami for 3.5 percent of what it cost John Paulson to get his kids into Harvard.

Grand total of expenditures so far, in round numbers: only $41.2 million.

Naturally, I'll give money to worthy causes. There are plenty of worthy causes. Such as my cousin Mikey-Mike. He spent Thanksgiving in jail after his seventh DUI arrest. It was just too cold to walk to the trailer park from the bar—half a block away. Maybe Mikey-Mike isn't a *very* worthy cause. But he is my cousin. I'll hire a designated driver for him. Or maybe just a big guy to carry him home.

I'll also donate to the local EMS. They were Johnny-on-the-spot at the accident scenes during Mikey-Mike's second, third, and fifth DUI arrests.

But I'm no "Give-It-Away Gates" or Warren "Leave-Air-to-the-Heirs Buffett." The problem with charity is that people can be remarkably hard to help. My cousin Mikey-Mike, for instance.

The other problem with charity is that you have to be careful when you try to make the world a better place.

When you try to make the world a better place, you're assuming that you know what the world needs, that you know what the world should be doing, that you know what everyone in the world wants. I don't even know what *I* want.

Furthermore, there's a danger in "sharing and caring." The danger is in the "caring" part. We're told we should *care*. Care about climate change, care about endangered species, care about the poor and oppressed.

But being terribly concerned about great big issues is a way of elevating yourself to membership in a self-selecting elite.

You care about climate change. You really, really care about climate change. You care so much it keeps you awake at night. You can hardly eat.

Meanwhile the rest of us just give $20 to the Sierra Club and forget about it.

You people who care so much are obviously superior to those of us who only care as much as we have to. And since you're such superior people, you have the right—nay, the duty—to tell all us other people (inferior people) what to do.

We inferior people may not buy that.

Nonetheless, I'll give $9,958,800,000 to worthy causes. Which, in addition to the $41,200,000 I've already spent, will bring my fortune down to a more manageable $90 billion.

Then, utilizing the remaining $90 billion, I'll do good with my money the old-fashioned way. By keeping it.

Let's say I keep my $90 billion in the most conservative fashion . . . No, not *that* conservative—$90 billion in gold bullion = approx. 4.8 million pounds of gold = one damn big hole I'd have to dig in my yard.

And I'm not putting it into U.S. Treasury bonds either. The last thing our fool government needs is somebody lending it $90 billion. Secretary Mnuchin would be skipping though the halls of the Treasury Building singing . . .

*The $82 billion deficit increase*
*Just got palmed with P. J. grease!*

No, let's say I put my money in twelve-month bank CDs at 1.25 percent interest. (True, this would require 360,000 different banks in order to keep my $90 billion fully FDIC-insured. That's about 356,000 more banks than there are in the U.S. But I guess I could start some new ones.)

An interest rate of 1.25 percent, paltry though it is, gives me an annual income of $1.125 billion. And even though I haven't invested in a way that any real investor would call "investing," my $90 billion is still out there in the world economy helping to increase global wealth.

An increase in global wealth is a good thing. Period. Even if you're up all night being a worrywart about climate change, you'd better realize that stopping or reversing or coping with the effects of climate change will require more wealth than the globe has now.

An increase in global wealth is the only certain way out of poverty and the only likely way out of oppression. With wealth comes power over the world. Men and women are freed from drudgery and exploitation. Businesses can be started, communities empowered, educations pursued, and cousin Mikey-Mike can buy a round of drinks.

Keeping my money will do good, even if I don't mean to.

And there's another way my money will do good. And I *really* didn't mean to do this. That is, pay taxes.

Gosh will I be doing that. I'll be in the top tax bracket—37 percent. That means an annual income tax bill of $337.5 million. Yes, all the money in the world will hire some excellent attorneys and accountants. And let's say I sail very close to the wind with the IRS. (I certainly intend to!) I'm still going to wind up being taxed a couple hundred million a year.

If I keep doing that for the rest of my natural life span, that will be more than $2 billion in taxes.

But let's look on the bright side. Even assuming that half my tax dollars go to "waste, fraud, and abuse," that's still a billion dollars' worth of paved roads and sewage treatment plants, of public education (with vouchers, I hope!), of benefits for veterans, the disabled, and my cousin Mikey-Mike, and of police and military protection for my fellow countrymen.

What if I simply give the $100 billion to the local chapter of Earth First! And then spend the next ten or a dozen years chained to an endangered ipe tree in the Amazon protesting illegal tropical rain-forest logging? How much good would that do?

For $100 billion I could have *bought* the rain forest.

# SECTION VI

## Random Walk

Phil Donahue: "What about the poor?"
Ayn Rand: "Don't be one of them."

> —Attributed to an interview with Rand on
> *Donahue* circa 1979 (not recorded in the
> transcript and probably apocryphal but,
> as we journalists say, "too good to check")

# Introduction

$A$ random walk goes nowhere in particular. Thus the theme of this section, which doesn't have one.

But "Random Walk" is also an important statistical concept. The phrase was coined by mathematician Karl Pearson (1857–1936), father of the modern discipline of statistics. And cursed be his name by all business majors being frog-marched through required courses in Statistics. (Pearson, the SOB, also invented the Standard Deviation.)

All "Random Walk" really means is that you have a formula or algebraical process the outcome of which is completely random. This turns out to be a surprisingly difficult thing to do in mathematics. (Just as it turns out to be a surprisingly easy thing to do in life.) A jollier term for it is "Drunken Walk," and all business majors who've managed to pass Statistics should treat themselves to one.

In economics the Random Walk is a key element of the "Efficient Market Theory" or "EMT." EMT asserts that the price of an asset (the usual example is a publically traded stock) reflects all the information available about the intrinsic value of that asset.

Therefore every asset is always "correctly priced" at any given time. And, because new information about the asset will be randomly favorable or unfavorable to the value of the asset, future changes of price will be a Random Walk and therefore impossible to predict.

In other words, if you're trying to figure out whether the stock market will go up or down, you're fucked.

Unless you're a genius and have an original way—that nobody else knows—of analyzing all the information available about the intrinsic value of an asset. You're not a genius. You're fucked.

With one exception. Efficient Market Theory fails to allow for the possibility that you are a liar, a thief, and a fraud. You may have presented information about an asset that's not true. You may be concealing "insider trading" information that you should have publically disclosed. You may be Bernie Madoff.

So, what EMT and Random Walk teach us is that the more honest you are, the less you know about what's going to happen next in business and economics.

And this makes me a really honest guy.

# Five Things I Know
# About China

Everybody's worried about China. The economic situation is complicated. But China isn't "the Mysterious East"; it's not impossible to understand.

A few years ago I traveled around China with two savvy companions, looking at the fabric of the Chinese economy and the nuts and bolts of China's economic growth.

I mean "fabric" and "nuts and bolts" literally. We spent our time at textile mills, steel mills, manufacturing plants, and clothing factories.

I was with old friends from Hong Kong—Tom, an engineer who's been in the steel business on the Chinese Mainland for thirty years, and Tom's wife, Mai, a Hong Kong native fluent in English, Cantonese, and Mandarin.

In 1980, when China was beginning its "Open Door" economic policy, Mai and her brothers started a textile machinery brokerage firm.

Mai's job was to take Mainland start-up entrepreneurs to Europe (where they encountered their first fork, escalator, etc.) and arrange for them to purchase used spinning, weaving, and dyeing equipment from the faltering textile companies of Belgium and France.

Tom, Mai, and I journeyed to Shanghai, Hangzhou, Nanjing, Wuxi, up the Yangtze River through the Three Gorges to Chongqing, north to Xi'an and Shaanxi Province, and south to Guangzhou.

Five things about China were clear:

1.  *The Chinese are more like Americans than anybody,
    including some Americans.*

As entrepreneurs the Chinese aren't just sharp, they're sharp-eyed, seeing opportunity where others see disaster.

Mr. Chen (I've changed the names of the people I interviewed) is a polyester fleece magnate who got his start as a soldier looking at Russian corpses during the 1969 Sino-Soviet border clash along the frozen Amur River.

He noticed the dead Russians had synthetic fabrics that were lighter and warmer than the fur the Chinese troops wore.

Mr. Chen knew nothing about textiles, but he convinced senior officers to let him start a small military research project.

When China went capitalist, Mr. Chen used his research to build a fleece business. The People's Liberation Army not only gave him permission, it provided financing.

But the secret to American-style capitalism is not only the success of good ideas, it's also the failure of bad ideas. Resilience is needed.

David, the tour guide and translator on our boat trip up the Yangtze, was the son of a truck driver. In the 1980s the Chinese government trucking monopoly began allowing drivers to lease trucks for 10 percent of profits.

David's mother scolded David's father for giving up his safe government job to lease a truck. But David's father wound up making $2,000 a year. "We had the first refrigerator in our neighborhood," said David.

Then David's family invested in the new, poorly regulated, easily manipulated Shanghai Stock Exchange. And lost everything.

"They moved to a small village," David said, "and worked all day and all night to start a tourist resort. Now they are prosperous again."

The Chinese work hard and play hard. I asked Mai why there weren't many Mainland Chinese on our cruise up the Yangtze. "They cruise *down* the Yangtze," she said. "It's three days instead of four, so they can have their fun faster. Mainlanders are always in a hurry."

And, Mainlanders also don't stint on hospitality. Tom and Mai's business friends outdid each other with umpteen-course meals. Tom calls it "death by banquet."

The Chinese like beer, wine, whiskey, and throat-searing *Maotai* sorghum brandy, and serve them all at the same time. You don't sip your drink in China. It's *gan bei* ("bottoms up") no matter the size of the glass.

The Chinese like to laugh. After four or five *gan bei* toasts at a banquet in Shanghai, Mr. Lui, a real estate developer, criticized America's involvement in Afghanistan.

I assumed we were talking politics and began mumbling nonsense that sounded like John Kerry.

"Don't talk politics," said Mr. Liu, "talk *price*. What do you spend on the war in Afghanistan? Maybe three hundred billion dollars? Maybe four hundred billion?" (In fact, the total, so far, is almost $900 billion.)

"Afghanistan," said Mr. Liu, "is twenty billion GDP. Has your president never heard of P/E ratio? Why not he *buy* the country from the Taliban?"

And China has a Frontier American egalitarianism. Every dinner included the business leader's secretaries, aides, assistants, and drivers, seated at the same table and eating, drinking, and talking with equal gusto. (Although the drivers were excused from *gan bei*.)

## 2. *China is a frontier.*

The wilderness begins just a few miles outside the cities. Although it's an economic wilderness. I didn't see any forests or prairies or wild animals.

A coal, coke, and iron ore broker from Xi'an, Mr. Tian, took me on a 150-mile trip to show off the coke oven he'd built in rural Shaanxi Province.

Except for a few high-tension wire towers and the highway, we saw what Marco Polo saw. Every bit of land was terraced to the hilltops. Even in burial grounds, crops grew right up to the gravestones.

The power from the power lines didn't reach the tiny villages, nor did the pavement or any water pipes. Goats, sheep, and pigs were few.

Mr. Tian grew up in one of these villages. China's subsistence agriculture, he said, doesn't produce the surplus needed to support domestic animals.

Average annual income in rural China was, at the time of my visit, about $620. Half of China's population is rural.

## 3. *China is still poor.*

This is good for investors. It shows how much growing China has left to do.

China's $10.4 trillion economy seemed huge—until I divided it by 1.3 billion Chinese.

China's per capita GDP was $13,224. Botswana's was $17,050.

China's government claimed the average wage was $8,575 a year. But it seemed to be a struggle to get a job with "average" pay.

In China's booming coastal cities I heard about "foreign workers" and "illegal immigrants." But I didn't see any workers who looked foreign except a few well-heeled expats.

Government permission is, technically, still needed to change your place of residence in China. The "foreign" illegal immigrants were from the country's own countryside.

The official minimum wage in China was $3,618 a year. For a Chinese family of four to reach the U.S. poverty line of $23,283, three adults would have to be working two full-time minimum-wage jobs each, plus overtime.

A few figures tell the story. But a look out the car window in Shaanxi told it better.

### 4.  *China's economic base is primitive.*

This is not good for investors. Because the problem is not old-fashioned machinery or out-of-date technology. The problem is a primitive, authoritarian, deeply corrupt, and highly arbitrary politico-economic system that lingers in China.

China's new factories were built with foreign capital to produce foreign exports. There's another side to Chinese manufacturing.

Tom took me to a Mao-era steel mill that his company bought from the Chinese government for $1, on the condition that Tom keep it operating.

The machinery *was* old-fashioned. Sir Henry Bessemer, who invented the Bessemer converter to mass-produce steel in 1856, would recognize every bit and piece of the mill.

What would have baffled Sir Henry was the two thousand workers Tom had to fire because they weren't doing any work. Not to mention the three hundred "ghost workers" who were on the mill's payroll and didn't exist at all.

The mill's workforce is now smaller than the number of ghosts it used to employ.

Tom had to cope with labor unrest. As we were climbing the tower to the blast furnace, Tom said, "Here's where a guy threw a wrench at me."

"What did you do?" I said. Tom was wearing an Armani suit, but he'd been a Ranger in Vietnam.

"I knocked him down the stairs," Tom said. "After that I got along fine with the workers."

There was also a family in the nearby village that, by tradition, had "theft rights" at the mill. They stole a railroad train full of iron ore. Tom caught them by following the train tracks.

Tom bought a 150-pound guard dog from the People's Liberation Army. Shasha ("Killer") was still there, delighted to see Tom and wagging a tail that could drive railroad spikes.

Tom's longest-running difficulty arose from a mill hand's having an affair with a woman working at the chemical factory next door. They got together in an electrical equipment closet. Midst throes of passion, the mill hand backed into high-voltage circuitry and was electrocuted. (His girlfriend survived—with her hair a bit more frizzy than is usual in China.)

The mill hand's widow brought her entire ancestral village to block the steel mill's gates. As compensation for her husband's death, she demanded his salary in perpetuity, a job for their mentally disabled daughter, a new house, and payment of her husband's gambling debts.

"I had to call in the Communist Party officials," Tom said.

"Did they ship her and her village to prison camp?" I asked.

"They didn't do anything. They said it was my problem. I finally settled with the widow for a couple hundred bucks."

### 5. China has a lot of history.

Some of it good. British scientist, historian, and China expert Joseph Needham maintained that from the first century B.C.

to the fifteenth century A.D., China was the most prosperous and technologically advanced country on earth.

Then progress stopped for five hundred years. The reason was an authoritarian, deeply corrupt, and highly arbitrary politico-economic system.

After the fall of the Qing Dynasty in 1911, China didn't recover. Instead, the Chinese Communists imposed a whole *new* authoritarian, deeply corrupt, and highly arbitrary politico-economic system.

Lately progress has been rapid. China's per capita GDP in 1980 was $310.

In Guangzhou I talked to Phillip, an American who moved to China to restore the antique furniture that had been wrecked and neglected by the Communists and to build reproductions using the original types of wood, tools, and finishes.

He showed me his workshop, where he runs a training program for young Chinese cabinetmakers.

Phillip said, "After a couple of generations when no one cared about craftsmanship, the craftsmanship is amazing."

I watched a young man making an intricate dovetail joint. Phillip explained that in European cabinetry there are five principal types of dovetail joints. But in Chinese cabinetry there are more than forty.

The young man was cutting the dovetail with a hatchet—a hatchet an American Boy Scout would use to split kindling while slicing off a toe.

Phillip said, "There is, however, a Chinese tendency to do things the hard way."

# Doubts About Asia

Not to be a wet Mao Suit, but . . .

I have my worries concerning Asia's future—its economic future and even its existential future.

What I don't doubt is that, in the near term, the Asian economy is going to grow like a bamboo shoot. Some species of bamboo can increase in height by thirty-six inches a day—an inch every forty minutes. If you set up your camp chair over a bamboo plant and take a snooze, you could be in for a surprise.

But just looking at Asia's economic growth without taking other factors into account can lead to the "Zero Baseline Fallacy."

The growth is extraordinary, but what's really extraordinary is where the growth started.

In 1978—only a moment ago in history—China's per capita GDP was $156.40.

China's per capita GDP has increased by 4,409 percent since then. But 4,409 percent of hardly anything is still not a whole bunch.

China's current per capita GDP is $6,895. America's current per capita GDP is $52,195.

Starting from a zero baseline is like the "Irish Fitness Program" joke that the Irish used to tell when Ireland was being a "Celtic Tiger."

### Irish Fitness Program

*Take two fifty-pound potato sacks and hold them out at arm's length.*

*Do this for one minute the first day, two minutes the second day, three minutes the third day, and so on, until you can hold the potato sacks at arm's length for an hour.*

*Now put one potato in each of the sacks.*

Furthermore, just looking at Asia's economic potential without taking other factors into account can lead to the "Chinese Arithmetic Fallacy."

China's economy is huge. But China is huge. There are 1.38 billion people in China. A number as gob-smackingly large as 1,380,000,000 can fog business thinking. Just 1 percent of China's population equals 13.8 million. Right now at Boeing HQ there's probably a group of top executives huddled in the boardroom telling each other, "If we could sell 787 Dreamliners to just one percent of . . ."

A more fundamental concern about Asia is democracy, or lack thereof. Several "Asia Experts" I've talked to have pointed out the "Command and Control" advantage that China, with its autocratic government, has over democracies such as the U.S. and India.

The advantage is real, but is it so advantageous?

Hitler improved Germany's depression-era consumer economy. But what ended up being consumed was Austria, Czechoslovakia, Poland, the Netherlands, Belgium, France, Denmark, Norway, etc.

Mussolini made the trains run on time. But where the trains were going was to take Italian troops to the front lines, where they would be slaughtered.

Democracy is slow and frustrating, but to discount democracy is to violate the Churchill maxim: "Democracy is the worst form of Government, except for all the others."

What democracy has going for it is that it's the only system under which there's a hope of preserving and expanding human rights. And the free market is, first and foremost, a human right. Economic liberty is inseparable from liberty itself.

A system such as China's, which allows citizens to trade in most physical objects but forbids them to trade in certain intellectual concepts, is like a system where everybody gets a car but nobody is allowed to learn to drive. Sooner or later there's going to be a crack-up.

Democracy is also the only safeguard against central planning. Central planning always looks efficient and expert—from a distance. But central planning always ends up with an "efficiency expert" deciding it would be more efficient if everyone wore the same size underpants, selected by an expert. I am hoping, for my sake, that that expert doesn't come over from the private sector at, say, Victoria's Secret. *A thong?* That's wrong.

Extended economic growth in democracies—particularly in English-speaking countries since the Industrial Revolution—beats anything on the historical record.

There isn't much of a democratic tradition in Asia. This is because of the barbarians.

*We're* the barbarians.

A certain rough democratic equality is common among barbarous peoples. It can be seen in the primitive tribes of the

Arctic, the Americas, the Antipodes, Africa, and most especially among the primitive tribes that invaded and conquered the Roman Empire, which would be us "Westerners."

*The fall of Rome we're taught to rue,*
*But it was we that Rome fell to.*

Civilization was born in Asia some nine thousand years ago. This means the people of Asia have—give or take—nine thousand more years of being civilized than we do. I have never spoken intimately to a person from Asia who did not consider Westerners to be barbarians (though the sentiment is usually expressed more politely than that).

And it's true. The World War II that the world had not long ago was based entirely on Western ideologies (including the fascism of Imperial Japan), and the worst tragedy that has befallen modern Asia—the gruesome depredations of Maoism—was also based on a Western ideology. We are guilty as charged.

But civilization has its discontents. Civilization leads to centralization, which leads to autocracy, which leads to absolutism. And absolutism is in absolute opposition to human liberty and human progress, whether absolutists know it or not.

Pol Pot knew it. Xi Jinping doesn't seem to.

I have other worries about Asia. The continent contains three major "Trip Wires of War." And that's not counting North Korea or the perpetually warring "Trump-word-holes" of the Middle East.

The least worrying is a U.S./China conflict. One of these countries has a grown-up for a leader. The other has a military led by grown-ups.

India/Pakistan is more of a 3 A.M. night sweat. India and Pakistan have already fought four wars since 1947, plus numerous military skirmishes and an ongoing armed standoff in Kashmir. Now they've both got nukes.

Pakistan could fall under control of Muslim extremists. India could fall under control of Hindu extremists. Whether you prefer paradise or endless reincarnation, you may get your wish. You and everybody else in the world.

Then there's poor, belligerent, unpredictable Russia sharing 2,600 miles of border with (relatively) rich, peace-inclined, orderly China. You remember what happened to Senator Rand Paul with his next-door neighbor.

I touched on religious extremism in Pakistan and India. But India has another problem besides Hindu extremism. India has the second-largest population of Muslims of any nation in the world—176 million versus Pakistan's 167 million. Then, sitting athwart trade routes, in the middle of everything, with the largest economy in Southeast Asia, is the country that has the very most Muslims, Indonesia—209 million.

The vast majority of Muslims are not interested in extremism, any more than the vast majority of Democrats are interested in knocking Rand Paul off his rider mower. The (no relation to Rand) RAND Corporation think tank regards Muslim extremists as being sort of like America's filthy rich (whom you're also unlikely to encounter personally). RAND estimates that less than 1 percent of Muslims worldwide are at risk of becoming radicals.

Yet, 176 million plus 167 million plus 209 million and add in the 21 million Muslims of China. That equals 573 million, times 1 percent . . .

So (the flip side of Boeing executives' hope for 787 sales), I've only got 5,730,000 people to worry about.

Then there are Asia's Failed States—always a danger to peace and prosperity, as the Failed States of Weimar Germany, Tsarist Russia, and the Confederate States of America proved.

The Philippines could become a Failed State, Myanmar seems to be trying to become one, and Afghanistan is already there. The former Soviet Republics of Central Asia—the "Trashcanistans"—all have Failed State potential. And, when it comes to a fully realized Failed State, North Korea takes the cake, or it would if it could get any cake-baking ingredients on the black market.

I don't fret much about what North Korea will do with its atomic bombs. Kim Jong-un is a murderer, not a suicide. But I don't like the example he sets in Asia and elsewhere.

Here's how to be the head of a Trump-word nation without any economy or cultural influence and no significant conventional military might and still be a huge player—a Harvey Weinstein (with the same weight-loss program)—in the theater of international relations. It sets a bad example.

However, in my doubts about Asia, I keep coming back to autocracy.

Well into Europe's Renaissance and the European Age of Discovery, China was still the richest and most technologically advanced nation in the world. Economic historians estimate that in the fifteenth and sixteenth centuries, China accounted for between 25 percent and 30 percent of the world's economy. By 1960 the figure was down to five percent. What happened?

Essentially just one thing—nothing.

During China's Qing Dynasty (1636–1912), China's autocrats decided to shut China off from commercial and intellectual contact with the outside world. Ships were burned. People were moved away from ports and coastal regions.

The Qing Dynasty's Qianlong Emperor, who ruled China for most of the eighteenth century, said, "Our land is so wealthy and prosperous that we possess all things. Therefore, there is no need to exchange the produce of foreign barbarians for our own."

My biggest concern for Asia is that some new autocrat will have the same thought—and the muscle to enforce his thinking.

# Thoughts While Cleaning the Chicken Coop

Recently I was shoveling shit in hell.

It was a hot day and I was performing my least favorite farm chore—the twice-a-year chicken coop clean-out.

This set me thinking while I shoveled . . . First, I thought about the phrase "I'd rather be shoveling shit in hell." I often use it in conversation.

**Friend:** "How'd you like to have Sarah Huckabee Sanders' job?"

**Me:** "I'd rather be shoveling shit in hell."

The expression is a cliché. But—I thought—clichés only become clichés because they express a truth. And the truth is I'd rather be cleaning out the chicken coop than . . .

Trying to sell Puerto Rican utility bonds.

Balancing the state budget of Illinois.

Negotiating Brexit.

Attempting to forge a just and lasting peace in the Middle East.

Be in the same room as Elizabeth Warren.

A cliché may be overused and trite. "Nobody loves you like your mother." But a cliché represents an idea we all agree on—and there aren't enough ideas we all agree on in America these days.

Maybe America should be more clichéd. Maybe we should have a society, a business world, and a political system based on clichés. I can think of some good ones.

All men are created equal.

They are endowed by their creator with certain unalienable rights.

Among these are life, liberty, and the pursuit of happiness.

Cleaning the chicken coop might seem to be an odd way of pursuing happiness. But I can tell you, from a certain amount of personal experience, that it's a better path to lasting joy than drink, drugs, and adultery.

The chicken coop wouldn't need to be cleaned out again for six months. With drink, drugs, and adultery, you can find yourself cleaned out the following morning.

Cleaning the chicken coop is also honest work, and when I'm done I've accomplished something (at least for the chickens).

This gives me more dignity than I have in most of the rest of my life—making fun of people for a living, being a second-string parent, failing to train my bird dogs, and taking eight strokes on a par 3 at the golf course (and that's after I've fudged my scorecard).

No one on earth has the right to look down on those who do honest work and accomplish something. Even if what they accomplish is a pile of chicken shit.

I may be filthy, sweaty, and stinking, but I rank higher in the aristocracy of life than people who do no work and accomplish nothing and much higher than the parasites who do dishonest work and suck the blood out of the accomplishments of others. This means that, compared with about 95 percent of America's elected officials, I am an imperial majesty—as long as I stick to cleaning my chicken coop.

Also, cleaning the chicken coop gives me an opportunity to do this kind of deep thinking. Mindless labor is a thought-provoking activity.

Not to compare my thinking to Einstein's, but I'll bet Einstein was doing something like cleaning a chicken coop when "$E=mc^2$" popped into his head.

(Actually he was working in the Swiss Patent Office. Which really does sound like shoveling shit in hell. Imagine day after day immersed in Germanically precise and detailed official documents concerning cuckoo-clock intellectual property.)

My thoughts ran to more prosaic subjects. Such as, "Where did all the shit come from?"

I have only eight chickens. They live in a large coop, about eight by twelve feet. The coop opens into an even larger pen, at least twelve by twenty. And every bit of the coop and the pen was covered in chicken shit.

Using a gravel rake and a garden spade, I filled my tractor bucket three times. That's enough to load a full-size pickup truck's bed to the brim.

As I delved and heaved, I began calculating the number of bags of layer-hen feed I buy; the frequency of my wife's giving the chickens vegetable trimmings, wilted lettuce, left-over Brussels sprouts, etc., and how long it had been since I last cleaned the coop.

*The chickens are pooping more than they eat!*

If the chickens were a business I was considering investing in, I'd smell something rotten. (Of course, in this case, I was smelling something rotten anyway.) When a corporation says it bought a ton of steel from which it manufactured two tons of steel widgets, I want to see the corporation's books.

My chickens don't keep books (so far as I know). But they're up to something.

Are they sneaking out of the coop at night and going to McDonald's? Maybe they're taking my car, with one chicken pecking the accelerator and another pecking the brake pedal while a third perches on the steering wheel. I should roll up the windows and quit leaving the keys in the ignition and my spare change in the cup holder.

I kept shoveling and had yet another thought. The chickens *are* a business. And I *did* invest in it. In fact, I invested quite a bit. There was the capital expense of building the coop and the pen, the cost of the chickens themselves, plus the cost of the chicken feed (the price of which is not, by the way, "chicken feed"). Then there's what I paid for the heated poultry waterer, the infrared lamp to keep the coop warm on freezing New England nights, the laying boxes, the feed trays, the feed scoop, and the mouse-proof feed bin. Not to mention what my feeding, water replenishment, egg collection, and coop clean-out time is worth, even figured at minimum-wage rates.

The return I get is one egg per day per hen (if she feels like it). Pricing that out, I figure each sunny-side up I have for breakfast sets me back about $1.50.

Even so, shoveling shit in hell turns out to be a good thing . . . in the following ways:

I got some exercise.

I did some deep thinking.

And I learned four important lessons about business and investing . . .

1.  Because people say the same thing over and over again doesn't mean it isn't true. There's no value in being contrarian just to be contrary.

2. Never undervalue honest work that accomplishes something, no matter how humble that something seems to
   be. This goes for employees and employers alike and
   for husbands, wives, friends, associates, chairmen of
   Fortune 500 companies, the people emptying those
   companies' wastepaper baskets, and *me*.

3. Be alert to mismatches between input and output. Take
   the Snapchat social media company as an example. Snapchat's output is supposed to be millions and millions in
   revenue. But Snapchat's input is just a bunch of social
   media or, as I would call it, "a pile of chicken shit."

4. Don't keep chickens.

# Six Lessons from a Man on Horseback

The key element of success for a person, a business, or a nation is to harness power and talent.

That's not a very original thought, but I was having it in a very appropriate place—atop a horse, where "to harness" is not just a metaphor.

Horses were domesticated perhaps as early as 3,500 B.C. The horse was the first large, self-activated thing that we humans brought under our control in order to increase our strength and force.

To this day we measure the output of most devices that produce strength and force in "horsepower." Therefore horses should offer us some lessons about harnessing power and talent.

Including our own. After all, though horses may outweigh us by half a ton, it was we who domesticated them, not the other way around. (Cowboys and Indians would have been a ridiculous conflict if horses had been mounted on Comanche and cattlemen.)

The reason I was atop a horse is that I spent a weekend staying with an old friend who has a horse farm in Virginia.

The visit was mostly for the benefit of my sixteen-year-old daughter, Lulu, who is an avid and accomplished horsewoman.

But she just goes around in circles in riding rings doing something called "dressage," which I believe is French for "dressed funny."

This is no way to appreciate the power and talent of horses.

My Virginia friend plays polo. My rural New England daughter had never seen polo played. We have plenty of horses and riders where we live. What we don't have is enough flat land for a polo ground, which is 300 yards long and 160 yards wide.

A polo ground is the size of nine football fields—large enough for all the NFL teams in the American Football Conference to play each other at the same time with room left over for a high school state championship.

(You should get a polo ground, if you want to harness an oversized lawn that otherwise just lies there.)

I once thought polo was nothing more than a punch line for jokes about rich people. Then, thirty years ago, I saw my first polo match. It's an amazing sport, a combination of rodeo trick riding, mounted golf, horse soccer, rugby on four legs, and the Super Bowl played with thousand-pound running backs.

And polo is the perfect place to see the harnessing of power and talent: watching everything a person and a horse can do together (well, not *everything*—polo is PG-rated) and how fast and how masterfully they can do it.

I wasn't playing. I was trotting around the periphery of the match, trying not to fall off. I love horses, but I'm a lousy horseback rider. I'm so bad I've fallen off a horse when it was standing still.

This can happen if you fail to tighten the saddle girth. A smart horse—and they're all smart when they feel like it—will puff itself up while you're putting on the saddle and then, when you're mounted, suck in its gut like me at the beach.

As a result the saddle spins around the way a whirligig lawn ornament does.

Thus the *First Business and Management Lesson from Horseback Riding*: Remember, when you're harnessing power and talent, whatever you're harnessing is probably more powerful and talented than you are (and more full of hot air).

Actually, that's the *Second Business and Management Lesson*. The first lesson is to think about how many failed riding start-ups there must have been.

People 5,500 years ago didn't know that a horse was the right thing to leap on the back of. I'll bet they were trying to leap on the back of all sorts of animals. They were jumping on giraffes, hopping on hippos, trying to mount mastodons and saber-toothed tigers. A lot of what was invested in these entrepreneurial initiatives must have resulted in a . . . so to speak . . . dead loss.

The *Third Lesson* is that people can be really determined to harness power and talent (e.g., trying to mount saber-toothed tigers) and, at the same time, be really stupid about it. Europeans had saddles for thousands of years, but it wasn't until the Middle Ages that it occurred to anyone to hang stirrups from those saddles.

Yes, you can ride without stirrups—if you have thighs like a pair of giant fleshy Vise-Grips. But Newton's Third Law of Motion—"For every action, there is an equal and opposite reaction"—suggests that when ancient Roman cavalry lances struck the shields of ancient Gauls, the Romans went backassward off their horses.

The *Fourth Lesson* is to give whatever you're harnessing a purpose in life. A machine without a purpose hardly qualifies as a machine. And a horse or a human without a purpose is a sad case. There's an old cowboy saying, "More people are killed by pet horses . . ." Meaning that your horse is more likely to do something stupid or vicious if it has no purpose. (The same, I suppose, could be said about husbands.)

Sure, horses and people are motivated by greed. Polo ponies want the feed bag and people want the string of polo ponies. But what *really* motivates man and beast is a goal. And a goal in polo will do. A horse's object of desire is to run like hell and dust it up with other horses in the herd. That's polo. Polo makes horses very happy—like cavalry battles used to. (Polo riders fall off almost as often as ancient Romans with lances.)

The *Fifth Lesson* is that you have to have the right equipment to harness power and talent. In horseback riding, oddly, "harness" is not what you call the thing you use for harnessing. You want a bridle. The most important part of a bridle is the bit. What the bit does is curb the horse's tongue.

If the above three sentences seem to apply to a certain person currently attempting to harness the power and talent of a presidential administration, that's not my fault.

This brings me to the *Sixth and Last Horseback-Riding Lesson.* As my daughter and my Virginia friend have been trying to tell me for years, the single and only secret of riding well is balance.

You have to have a gut feeling for where you are on the horse. (For me it's more like a "butt feeling," and a sore one at that.)

Overachievers, business leaders, and, in particular, holders of high political office are not famous for always keeping their balance.

The phrase "Man on Horseback"—meaning a proud, vain politician who thinks he's the savior of his nation—was coined to describe the nineteenth-century French politician General Georges Ernest Boulanger. He was a provocative, mouthy, reactionary nationalist with a strong appeal to working folks.

During the 1880s Boulanger was so popular in France that French lefties were practically wetting themselves for fear that he'd declare himself dictator.

Boulanger made almost all of his public appearances mounted on a horse. I suppose there were situations where this looked silly, such as inside the French Chamber of Deputies. But appearing in public on horseback does produce a more imposing effect than appearing in public on Twitter.

I'm not being partisan here. Our previous chief executive thought he was the savior of the nation too. He was a provocative, mealymouthed, pinko internationalist with a strong appeal to folks who have no intention of working.

That guy should have realized that appearing on horseback produces a more imposing effect than appearing on *Comedians in Cars Getting Coffee*.

Of course, whether we *want* our presidents to be more imposing . . . that is, to impose on us even more than they do already . . . is another question.

Maybe presidents should take their riding lessons from me.

# Sympathy for
the Devil

I was about to launch into strong invective about the "antifas," those noisy young creeps trampling on liberty, vandalizing property, and assaulting those whose political opinions they deem "incorrect" . . .

Then I realized I was one of them. Or had been. Or had tried to be.

It was a long time ago—fifty years. But in 1968 I was as noisy, as young, and as much of a creep as anybody plaguing the streets of Berkeley today.

Why?

Because it was fun.

Not that I would have admitted this at the time.

Ostensibly, the reason I was out trampling, vandalizing, and assaulting was to protest the war in Vietnam.

The government of the United States wanted to send me to a distant place with noxious flora and fauna and shoot people I didn't even know. And what's more, those people were going to shoot back.

It wasn't that I was a pacifist.

If the government had wanted to send me *home*, to shoot my stepfather while the drunken bum was asleep on the couch, I would have willingly enlisted.

As it was, however, the war in Vietnam seemed like a good thing to protest.

And here I feel for the antifas. They are protesting . . . What *are* they protesting? Pretty much everything you can think of. Which is to say nothing much. It must be hard getting a bunch of real jerks together for no real reason. That's probably why, fifty years ago, there were so many more of us pasty-faced peace creeps than there are black-masked antifa creeps today.

I also feel bad for the antifas because, from what I can tell peeking beneath the hoodies and behind the bandannas, their angry, empowered women aren't nearly as cute as our hippie chicks were.

But to return to the more destructive kinds of fun . . .

Once we started protesting against the war in Vietnam we realized that . . . "Rioting—it's a riot!" And the war became simply a good excuse for having one.

There was excitement! There was camaraderie! There was derring-do!

I was, I confess, never really very good at rioting. I weighed only about 130 pounds in those days, so any liberties I trampled were trampled upon lightly.

I was too fundamentally middle class to be much of a vandal. I was pretty sure that if I smashed a store window my mother would pop up out of nowhere, snap a dish towel at me, and yell, "Windows don't grow on trees! They cost money! Somebody worked hard to make the money for that window! And it's coming out of *your* allowance!"

My "allowance" in 1968 was pretty much contained in a baggie of pot that was down to stems and seeds and probably wouldn't go far toward paying for a store window.

As for assaulting, I remember a lot more running *away* from the police than charging *at* them. Still, if you were quick enough in your retreat to give yourself a moment to turn around and (from a distance) shout at the "pigs" . . .

*Ho, Ho, Ho Chi Minh*
*The NLF is gonna win!*

It would impress those hippie chicks.

Then the better kind of fun began. "Oh wow, Sunshine! We're covered in tear gas! Let's go back to the crash pad. And—since we have to conserve the earth's resources—we'd better double up in the shower."

I suppose things are much the same today as they were fifty years ago. Though tear gas is more romantic than pepper spray, which is best washed off with vinegar. (But I understand that many of the antifas are vegans, so they're used to smelling like a salad.)

And I expect things will end much the same way as they did fifty years ago.

I remember when I stopped being a noisy young creep trampling on liberty, vandalizing property, and assaulting those whose political opinions I deemed incorrect. It was Monday, May 4, 1970.

That was the day the National Guard shot thirteen people just like me, killing four of them, at Kent State University in my home state of Ohio.

I was off at graduate school in Baltimore. But my high school girlfriend Connie Nowakowski was there in the fired-upon crowd. And the National Guard could have shot that innocent Catholic girls' school girl's adorable, faintly activist butt off.

They weren't shooting at Abbie Hoffman and Jerry Rubin. They were shooting at *us*.

And it was an irony—not lost on me even at the time—that the Kent State protesters had actually shot *themselves*. That is, the same ordinary middle-class adolescent Ohioans who were in the National Guard to avoid the draft shot the same ordinary middle-class adolescent Ohioans who were at Kent State to avoid the draft.

So, antifas . . . Drop the hoodie hood, turn the bandanna around, and get a job.

# Reform or Deform?

## On Fixing the Government

Government "reform" is something we hear a lot about, and always have. Let's quit listening. The guiding principle of government is to exercise power over the governed. The driving force of government is to acquire more of that power. No "reform" is going to eliminate these governmental mainsprings.

We can, with our electoral powers, limit government. We can, with our constitutional rights, resist government. What we cannot do is reform government in the dictionary definition sense of "reform": "to make better by removing faults and defects."

Government *is* a fault and a defect.

In a perfect world, where mankind was good and the universe was beneficent, there would be no need for government.

That isn't the world we live in.

Mankind being notso-hotso and the universe being a harsh and unforgiving place, maybe it's only to be expected that most "government reforms" make government worse.

For example, consider the following five commonly proposed modest (that is to say, not on the scale of Obamacare) government reforms. Note how they would tend to *deform* rather than *reform* our government and our society.

## Campaign Spending Limits
## (And its evil twin, "Publicly Funded Elections")

This is a bad kind of reform and calls for it are a waste of bad breath. Campaign spending limits simply can't happen.

First, as it were, there's the First Amendment—protecting campaign free speech like Cerberus the giant three-headed dog guarding the gates of Hades.

Attempt any real limitation of that campaign free speech and one of Cerberus's three heads—the executive, the legislative, or the judicial—will bite your ass.

Second, there is a law of physics. As the journalist Jonathan Alter, a self-confessed liberal/progressive, put it in a 1997 article in *Newsweek*, "Money in politics is like water running downhill: It will always find its way, even with a constitutional amendment."

And what if we did manage to limit campaign spending, including spending by issue-oriented groups supposedly not endorsing a specific candidate? Then the loudest cheapskate candidate with the dumbest, meanest slogan would win: "Soak the Rich!" or "Make America Great Again!" or some combination of both.

With campaign financing, as with so many distasteful aspects of politics and government, the best we can hope for is a bit of transparency in the disgusting soup. If some candidate is getting billions of dollars from "The Intergalactic Association of People Who Have Been Abducted by Aliens," I, for one, would like to know about it.

## Balanced Budgets, Spending Freezes, Debt Caps, Etc.

No law concerning such things will ever be written without some provision for nullification during a "National Emergency."

And, within days of the law's passage, we'll have a "National Emergency." (The emergency will probably be something on the order of discovery of invasive Asian carp in Lake Michigan.)

The government controls the supply of the money government spends. Government has too many ways to replenish its supply of spending money—taxing, borrowing, and printing more of the stuff. As for stopping the government from spending that money, see Jonathan Alter quote, above.

## Term Limits

Yes, the career politician is a problem. And so is every other kind of politician.

The more so because politicians—especially at the municipal level and in the House of Representatives—tend to be elected by pressure groups that dominate their constituencies. If the pressure group elects Clarabell and Clarabell limits out, the pressure group will elect Bozo. And when Bozo can't run anymore, Pennywise from *It* will be ushered into political office.

Nor are "outsider" candidates, with no political experience, a perfect answer. (We've got one now, in the White House.) Do you want a dog that knows where the bones are buried? Or do you want a dog that digs up the *whole* yard?

## Increasing Federal Aid to Public Education

The federal government originally became involved in local public schools with the "Elementary and Secondary Education Act of 1965," part of LBJ's "War on Poverty." The federal government has been getting more and more involved ever since.

Here, from the College Board's own SAT test figures, is the evidence for how helpful federal government involvement has been:

*Average SAT scores, 1967*
Reading/Verbal: 543
Math: 516

*Average SAT scores, 2016*
Reading/Verbal: 494
Math: 508

It's not a partisan matter. Republican aid to public education has been every bit as bad as Democratic aid to public education.

For example, George W. Bush's "No Child Left Behind." What if they *deserve* to be left behind? What if they deserve a *smack* on the behind? A nationwide testing program to determine whether kids are . . . What? Dumb? You've got kids. Kids are dumb.

And so's the government. Yet there seems to be no way out of dumb (dumb to the tune of $40 billion a year) federal aid to public education.

Imagine the fate of the politician running for national office who stood up and said, "No, I *can't* fix public education. The problem isn't funding or overcrowding or teachers' unions or voucher programs or lack of computer equipment in the classroom. The problem is *your damn kids!*"

## Passing "Living Wage" Legislation

Nice idea. But why stop at a paltry $15 an hour? Why not make the minimum wage $500 an hour, like the billing rate at white-shoe law firms? We'd all be millionaires, the way fancy lawyers are.

Oh, voters would perceive a problem with that? They'd realize that a $5.99 Big Mac Meal would cost about fifty-five times as much? They'd think $329.45 was a lot to pay for a burger, fries, and a Coke?

Then it's time for voters to realize that the same problem applies to a $15-an-hour minimum wage. The law of supply and demand means that, practically speaking, you can't raise the price of labor above what people are willing to be paid to work.

The difficulty is not so much that an overly high minimum wage will destroy small businesses with marginal profit rates and increase unemployment. (Though it will.)

The real problem is that people who are willing to work for less and businesses that can't pay more will be driven under the table, will become a part of the black market economy.

A black market economy turns otherwise innocent people into criminals, produces no tax revenues, and leaves everyone involved—including employees—without the protection of rule of law.

Note what happened during Prohibition. Note what's happening in the illegal drug market now.


## REAL REFORM

But let's not despair. There *are* ways government can be "made better by removing faults and defects." Some of the faults and defects are so obvious that even government itself could remove them.


### Tax Reform

Don't get your hopes up. The recent "sweeping tax reforms" (deformative though they may be) will probably get swept away again by continued partisan brawling. But there *is* the federal corporate tax rate, now reduced to 21 percent. Perhaps some legislative wisdom will prevail and this will be kept at a low level.

The U.S corporate tax rate used to be 35 percent (the highest in the industrialized world).

The worldwide average corporate tax rate is 22.96 percent.

Europe's average corporate tax rate is 18.35 percent.

Ireland's corporate tax rate is 12.5 percent. (Is the Irish economy's amazing recovery from the Great Recession a mere coincidence?)

China's corporate tax rate is 25 percent. (But can be discounted to as little as 15 percent for "government-encouraged" industries. Can you spell D-U-M-P-I-N-G?)

Was the U.S. corporate tax rate of 35 percent competitive? Were the Cleveland Browns?

## Tort Reform

Four possible quick fixes that would help us say goodbye to "Litigation Nation":

1.  Institute a "Loser Pays" tort system. The loser of a lawsuit pays the legal fees of the winner plus all court costs. This should make people think twice before they sue Dairy Queen for the pain and emotional distress of getting a "brain freeze" due to DQ's ice cream being too cold.

2.  Eliminate class-action suits. We're a nation of individuals, not a Marxist country full of "classes" at war with each other.

3.  Limit damages to what can be materially proven. The "brain freeze" was so bad that you dropped your ice cream. For your damages you receive a melted sundae. (If the jury insists on punitive damages because the defendant is a very terrible person, corporation,

or institution, the money should go into the taxpayer kitty.)

4. Limit lawyer fees to 5 percent of materially proven (not punitive) damages awarded. Being a lawyer is horrible, but it's only 5 percent as horrible as being badly injured enough to bring a tort suit under conditions 1–3.

## Kill the Gerrymander

Too many seats in Congress and state legislatures are "safe seats." They're always held by either a conservative Republican or a liberal Democrat, because the voting districts are shaped like something that lives under a rock. The voting districts slither all over the map to make sure they include a majority of one kind of voter. The other kinds of voters never have anybody to vote for. As a result we have no opportunity for real (small-d) democratic debate.

Math is the answer! Get a panel of math geeks and make sure they have no interest in or knowledge of partisan politics by asking them two questions.

If their answers to the two questions are . . .

"A **Trump** is any playing card of a suit that ranks higher than other suits during the playing of a hand in a card game."

And . . .

"Sir Edmund **Hillary**, born July 20, 1919, died January 11, 2008. In 1953 he and Tenzing Norgay became the first climbers confirmed to have reached the summit of Mount Everest, which has an altitude of 8,848 meters, or 29,029 feet."

Then we've got the right folks.

Instruct them to redraw all U.S. voting districts to include the same number of voters within each of the most compact and regular possible two-dimensional Euclidian geometric figures.

### Regulatory Two-for-One

On January 30, 2017, President Trump signed an executive order requiring that for every new federal regulation instituted, two must be rescinded.

And that's an *order!*

### Ourselves

Then there is what's ultimately at the root of every bad thing about government. Those who are in charge of the political system will submit to any indignity, perform any vile act, do anything to achieve and expand their power. Every government is a parliament of whores.

The trouble is . . . And I've been saying this for more than twenty-five years but apparently I need to keep saying it . . . In a democracy, the whores are us.

# Free-for-All!

I woke up one autumn morning and everything was free.

All goods and services were now completely free. It had to be true, because the clock radio came on and even NPR was giving away tote bags without begging for donations.

I rolled over in bed, happily mulling a list of things I want—*And could get without paying for them!* A Learjet . . . A 1955 Mercedes 300SL Gullwing coupe . . . in silver . . . with the black and white plaid racing seats . . .

Come to think of it, send all the kids to Harvard. If everything's free, then, presumably, 800 SAT scores are free too.

And, best of all, with no need for a paycheck, I could take the day off.

I got up whistling a merry tune, pulling on my pants and thinking, "Soon these trousers will be the bottom half of a bespoke Savile Row suit."

Over a leisurely breakfast, I pondered the question, "What armload of the earth's priceless bounty (now literally *priceless*) should I gather unto my bosom?"

Fortunately, our family is pretty well-off. There isn't anything we desperately *need*. No expensive operation for crippled little Timmy or anything like that. And none of our kids are named Timmy anyway.

We live out in rural New England. Like most country folks, we're well-provisioned this time of year. Our pig's been slaughtered and is in the freezer, along with half a beef cow from the farmer down the road (and a whole bunch of frozen pizza just in case we get down to tongue, tripe, and pig's feet).

The wood is stacked. The furnace oil has been topped up. Cars, truck, and tractor are in running order. Old fridge in the basement is stocked with beer. Got jerry cans of diesel for the generator. If the neighbors use up so much free electricity that the kilowatts coming out of our wall sockets go down to a trickle, no problem.

I could take my time deciding what no-cost, complimentary, on-the-house stuff I should go out and get first.

Funny how old habits die hard. My immediate thought was, "Money." I forgot that money was of no further use. I drove to the bank in town to get a couple of trash bags full.

Guess the bank tellers forgot too. They'd taken it all and left the bank vault open and the safety deposit drawers pulled out. Nothing in there but some bearer bonds and stock certificates littering the floor.

No use for those anymore. Although Berkshire Hathaway did look attractive at $0.00 per share. Of course, it would never pay a divided again. But it never paid a dividend before.

As long as I was I town, might as well pick up some groceries gratis. Seems like a lot of people had the same thought. And they weren't returning their grocery carts to the cart rack or parking between the lines in the parking lot. In fact, somebody had backed his pickup truck through the automatic sliding doors and was throwing cases of Samuel Adams Boston Lager into the pickup bed. He probably should have stuck to Bud in cans, because the Sam Adams bottles were bursting all over the place. It was a mess.

It was a worse mess inside the grocery store. Squealing children, faces smeared with chocolate, swarming the candy aisle. Housewives rooting though the produce bins, tossing bruised fruit and wilted vegetable over their shoulders. Grown men running and blocking and tackling each other with T-bone steaks as the football and the meat cooler as the line of scrimmage.

All I wanted was a little cheese—a wheel of Stilton, fat wedge of Parmigiano Reggiano, large Brie de Melun, ten pounds or so each of Roquefort, Gruyère, Gorgonzola, Mozzarella di Bufala, Camembert de Normandie, and Molitero Black Truffle Pecorino. You know, the kind of stuff that makes the snack tray look special. We already had saltines at home.

But I never got to the deli counter. Some old folks had commandeered the shuttle from the local retirement community. Gosh, they were spry. There was a pink-haired lady in a walker swinging a kielbasa. She would have been batting .400 for the Astros if she was playing MLB.

Things were every bit as bad at the gas station. Tug-of-war with the pump hoses. People using the fuel nozzles like nunchucks. Then somebody started squirting high-test at other folks because they were trying to pull him away from his boat trailer, where he was filling the 130-gallon fuel tank on his Bertram 24 Sport Fisherman. Good thing nobody smokes anymore.

### KA-BOOM!!!

*Almost* nobody smokes anymore.

Let's not even talk about what was going on at the liquor store. Though I did manage to get away with a couple of bottles of 2010 Châteauneuf du Pape. The locals thought 2010 was the sell-by date.

Everywhere I looked in this heretofore peaceful, sleepy little town there was—as that gloomy old political philosopher Thomas Hobbes called it—a "war of all against all."

Made me think. Communist countries are based on the idea that everything is free. In *The Communist Manifesto* Karl Marx says, "The theory of the Communists may be summed up in the single sentence: Abolition of private property."

No wonder communist countries are brutal dictatorships. It would take a lot of totalitarianism and secret police and gulags and so on to control that old lady clubbing me with a kielbasa. Gives you sympathy for Kim Jong-un.

I decided to go home.

This is the part of a polemical fiction where I need to make an expository speech, like the speech of copper baron Francisco d'Anconia in Ayn Rand's *Atlas Shrugged*, about money being the root of all *virtue*.

Ideally the writer works such speeches in as part of a dialogue. But the other person in the dialogue—in my case, my wife—doesn't get to say much. (In *Atlas Shrugged* Francisco goes on for five pages in response to a snide remark by hateful anticapitalism journalist Bertram Scudder. I shall try to contain myself.)

"Oh my gosh, what happened to you?!" asked my wife.

"Money is the root of all virtue," I replied. "Goods and services *shouldn't* be completely free. For years now we have been treating goods and services as if they were *de facto* free. It was only a matter of time before we made them free *de jure*.

"It started in the 1920s," I said, "with easy access to consumer credit on the installment plan—'Buy Now, Pay Later.' This didn't make goods and service free, of course, but it made goods and service almost *seem* free.

"Customers no longer had to save up money to pay for what they wanted with cold hard cash. (Which even paper money was in those days, being backed with gold and silver that are cold and hard.)

"My Dear," I went on to say, "that was just the beginning of a long-term trend—I would even call it a plot—to separate *the desire to purchase* from *the duty to pay*.

"By the 1930s individual stores were issuing charge plates so that wives could buy finery one month and not let husbands find out until the following month . . ."

"Ahem," my wife interrupted. "I'm the one who balances the checkbook around here . . ."

"In 1950," I continued without pausing, "Diners Club introduced a general use 'credit card' that allowed cash-free purchases at restaurants and a wide variety of other commercial establishments. In 1958 the American Express card promoted this 'un-pay' concept worldwide.

"Our own children have no idea what things cost or how the cost is met. Our children will say, 'Sorry I sat down on the glass-top coffee table and my butt busted it to pieces. But you can just go on Amazon and get another one.'

"Now people can simply tap their iPhones on something to go into debt. Debt, incidentally, that the events of this very day have shown will never be paid. What has the world come to?"

"Well," said my wife, "If you'd 'come to' a little earlier this morning, we could have gotten a new Whirlpool washer and dryer from Sears for nothing."

"No," I said, "we could *not*. Sears has already been put out of the appliance business—effectively put out of all business—by Internet commerce, with its false and deceiving promises of free goods and services."

"Free Goods and Services"—that was the lead story on all the television news channels. The whole country was going crazy just like my little town. Except in the big cities, where everybody is crazy anyway and things were much worse.

Niketown on 57th Street in Manhattan had run out of the new $230 Nike Air Foamposite Pro model. And a mob was hanging store clerks from the fire sprinklers with shoestrings. Or trying to. A lot of Nike shoes use hook and loop fasteners, and it's hard to lynch a person with Velcro.

Got to hand it to the TV newscasters, staying on the air for free. Some people would rather be a big cheese on the TV screen than have anything else. But I noticed that the TV stars were operating the cameras and the microphone booms themselves. Not everybody is stupid enough to rather be famous than rich.

Too bad about that Learjet I wanted. I saw on television that all the pilots of everything that will fly have flown away to someplace where you can still get a price for an airplane— mostly the top drug-smuggling countries, where I understand that market principles are still operating as usual.

By afternoon I was tired of the news and went down to my henhouse. The eggs there have *always* been free.

But my eggs were gone, and so were my chickens.

That's when I heard the noise in my hilltop hay field. Drove my truck up there and thirty acres of timothy and clover had been smashed flat by RVs, camper vehicles, and travel trailers.

Have to admit there *is* a spectacular view from that spot. Glad I got the hay in before everybody arrived.

Some of my uninvited guests were chopping my trees for firewood. Some were hauling drinking water out of my trout stream while, upstream, others were emptying their RV waste tanks into the brook. A number of familiar-looking chickens were roasting on BBQ grills.

I shouted at the crowd. But they'd been working hard on the bottles of Sam Adams that hadn't smashed when they were thrown into the pickup bed at the grocery store, and they were making too much noise for me to be heard.

I climbed up on the roof of my truck cab and, at the top of my lungs, implored the people to leave. I begged and pleaded with them to leave. I offered to pay them to leave.

"Your money's no good here!" said a great big drunk guy.

And, considering that morning's sudden change in the American economic system, he had a point.

So I went home, got out a key, and opened the one room in my house that's kept locked. (That said, *all* the doors and windows will be locked and bolted from now on.) Then I spun the combination on the cabinet safe . . .

If everything is going to be free, then there is going to be a new way of paying for things.

I silently thanked my old friend and fellow foreign correspondent, Leon, for what he'd told me so many years ago in Somalia. I put fifteen rounds in the magazine and slipped the magazine into my 9mm Glock—VISA card of the future.

Better to go down dignified
With boughten friendship at your side
Than none at all. Provide, provide.

—Robert Frost, "Provide, Provide"

# Acknowledgments

## *Funny Business*

It is only fit that a book devoted to not taking business too seriously should have its genesis in fun.

In August 2014 I gave a speech at a conference in Las Vegas hosted by the investment advisory firm Stansberry Research. I met Stansberry founder Porter Stansberry, General Manager Jamison Miller, and Stansberry's top analysts. They were smart and they were enjoying themselves. Likewise, Stansberry's clients. We had a lot of food, drink, and fun. (And—a sidelight on people who understand math and statistics—hardly anyone gambled.)

Stansberry is a publishing company specializing in information about and analysis of finance and economics. It produces a score of newsletters and numerous books, video conferences, and podcasts devoted to investment insights.

I realize that I am not the person to be giving advice on investment advice. I was an English major or, as they call it in business school, stupid. The best investment I've made lately? I left a $20 bill in my suit jacket pocket when I took my wife out for dinner on Labor Day weekend, and I found it this morning.

I'm probably too stupid to talk about business. But, in fairness to myself, I'm not just stupid. I am a *student* of stupidity. I'm a political reporter.

I may not be competent to talk about anything else, but I am fully competent to talk about politics. I've been covering the stuff for forty-eight years. After decades of mucking through politics you become aware that it is a business—a bad business, but a business nonetheless. It's not just a matter of the net greed in gross campaign contributions. Politics has a strong economic component even (maybe especially) when the pay comes in the form of power rather than pelf.

The original term for the interaction of government, money, and law, coined in the seventeenth century, was "political economics"—a disciple grounded in the study of Moral Philosophy. And, gosh, politics and economics should go back to Moral Philosophy and study harder.

Anyway, a half-decent political reporter always ends up as an amateur economist. In this capacity I did my due diligence before speaking at the Las Vegas event.

Stansberry's investment advice seems solid by my modest lights. More importantly, the information and analysis Stansberry generates isn't home to any of the "Four Horsemen of the Personal Finance Apocalypse."

Fraudulence
Stupidity
Dead Wrong Ideas
M.O.T.O. – Mastery of the Obvious

I gave my speech: "Pirates In Neckties – Business or Government, Which Is Worse?" Later that year Porter and Jamison invited me to speak at another Stansberry event in the Dominican Republic. We had more fun. We went deep-sea fishing. I spoke again at Stansberry's August 2015 Las Vegas conference. That fall Porter asked me if I'd like to write a weekly column in his *Stansberry Digest* newsletter.

I said, "Porter, you know I don't know anything about business."

Porter said, "You know funny business when you see it."

Then, in 2017, Porter started a free web magazine, *American Consequences*, to give Stansberry analysts and other writers a wider scope for financial commentary, economic investigation, and political inquiry. He asked me to edit it. And Jamison sketched all the plays on the blackboard.

It's been fun. This book is a collection of columns, articles, and essays I've written for the *Stansberry Digest* and *American Consequences*. Thank you, Porter.

And thank you, *American Consequences* staff. ("Staff" being a euphemism for people who do all the work.)

Editorial Director Carli Flippen provides genius. Managing Editor Steven Longenecker brings more of it. Creative Director Erica Wood has, with further genius, created the world's first web page designs that don't look like they were designed by web page designers (sitting in their moms' basements wearing pajamas and acne cream). Assistant Editors Chris Gaarde and Laura Greaver give much more than assists in their fresh, clean, and pellucid editing. Newswire Editors C. Scott Garliss, John Gillin, and Greg Diamond return with record catches when they troll the murky depths of modern media. And Sam DeCroes, Jared Kelly, and Jill Peterson sell our ads and are a reminder to us: "All of life is selling." It's when we die that you say, "He bought it."

*American Consequences* has been blessed with vital, vivid, vivacious—all the invigorating words starting with V but none of the V hand gestures post-Churchill—contributors: Hank Blaustein, Doug Casey, Peter Churchouse, Tama Churchouse, Turney Duff, Nicholas Eberstadt, Dr. David Eifrig, Andrew Ferguson, Kim Iskyan, Mary Kuntz, Alice B. Lloyd, Victorino Matus, John Podhoretz, Christine Rosen, Rahul Saraogi, Buck Sexton, Bill Shaw, Steve Sjuggerud, and more.

Also a blessing has been a chance to work with many of the other people at Stansberry Research, including—but not limited to—CEO Mark Arnold and Justin Brill, Justin Dove, Dan Ferris, Sean Goldsmith, Sam Latter, Dan Ostrowski, and Mike Palmer.

And every night the publishing house Grove Atlantic is in my prayers, "Forgive us our book advances."

Saintly Associate Editor Allison Malecha shaped this mess of an ill-typed, misspelled, grammatically challenged, and factually approximate manuscript into a form that closely resembles a book. Managing Editor Julia Berner-Tobin took the flood of words, pile of literary lumber, and rows of similes two-by-two and made them into an ark that will "set sale." Director of Publicity Deb Seager, famous director that she is, raised her megaphone and demanded, "Lights! Camera! Action!" Publicity Manager Justina Batchelor managed somehow—even though the book has not been the subject of a White House lawsuit and the author hasn't, as far as he knows, been indicted by a grand jury—to get us publicity. Rights Manager Erica Nunez protected our First Amendment right to charge for free speech. Art Director Gretchen Mergenthaler, with her masterful artistry, directed the art. (Please *do* judge this book by its cover.) Copyeditor Tom Cherwin, faced with a Labor of Hercules in cleaning the Augean Stable of my prose, did not shirk but diverted [his/her] rivers of learning and knowledge to wash away the dung in my scribblings. Wizard photographer James Kegley's work graces the cover. (Observe the dynamic composition, the subtle play of light and shadow, James can't help the subject.) And Scott Manning of Scott Manning and Associates—publicists to the stars, also me—was Vigil to my hapless Dante on book tour. ("I found myself within a dark talk show where the straight way was lost.")

There are many others to whom I owe thanks. Michael Farr, CEO of Farr, Miller & Washington, manages our family finances in conjunction with my too-smart-to-be-an-English

NONE OF MY BUSINESS

major wife. Left to my own devices I'd hand over our savings to this "Mernie Badoff" guy I've been hearing about who runs Federal Corrections Institution Medium-Security Investments LLC in Butner, North Carolina.

Then there are those who are willing to listen to me natter about economics without laughing out loud. Thank you Jay Caauwe, Stacey Hadash, Ed Mallon, Michael Meehan, and Nick Silitch. You are good friends all.

Something that anti-capitalists will never understand about business is how much of the free market is a friendship.

Let me note that by friendship I don't mean a cabal or secret society of top-hatters carrying moneybags and ruling the world by meeting in Davos. Let me also note that by anti-capitalists I mean people across the political spectrum—from the increasingly friendless man in the Oval Office to the un-friendly mob protesting him.

What I'm talking about is that the free market depends on trust. And that business depends far more on cooperation for mutual benefit than competition for lonely winner-take-all profit. It was the original superhero of the free market, Adam Smith, who pointed out that whenever A trades with B both gain. Each has given the other something that he values less in return for something that he values more. You might even call it love. I surrendered my bachelor license for wedded bliss and my wife forfeited her unmarried liberty for (and here the analogy breaks down somewhat) me.

Let's stick with friendship, to which I owe this book. First there are my friendships—now going on what's called life-long—with my editor and publisher Morgan Entrekin, president of Grove Atlantic, and my lecture agent Don Epstein, CEO of Greater Talent Network Speakers Bureau.

Morgan and I met in the late 1970s when he was a young book editor looking for books to publish and I was a young magazine editor looking to publish a book. The indomitable Elaine Kaufman—proprietor of Elaine's and friend to all in the lit biz—said, "You two do a book together." (Which command may have had something to do with the large restaurant tabs she had allowed us both to run up.)

Don and I met not long after. He had a fledgling speakers bureau and was trying to find speakers. I had a fledgling freelance career and was trying to not starve. We had the same lawyer—and friend—Mort Janklow. Mort said, "You two talk." (Which command may have had something to do with the large legal bills he had allowed us both to run up.)

The innocent cynic says, "It's not what you know, it's who you know." The experienced businessperson says, "It's what you know about who's your friend."

Through Don, I became friends with GTN Senior Vice President David Buchalter whose job is to befriend business people who want their friends, the clients, to have a friendly speaker at business events. David's other job is to be—in a friendly way—tough as Bill Belichick in negotiating what the speaker (me!) gets paid. Negotiation is what David does for fun (combined with golf).

Which brings us full circle to my meeting my Stansberry Research friends (with whom David ended up golfing a lot).

This is another thing that anti-capitalists will never understand about business. Capitalism is fun. Big fun. Even more fun than golf. You're out there with your team, blocking losses, tackling profits, connecting with the long ball or throwing an interception, making incredible yardage on third-and-impossible or punting when you have to, and how well you're doing is visible on the scoreboard.

Anti-capitalists are playing hacky-sack.